Author of the bestseller *The Source*
SIRSHREE

SECRET OF HAPPINESS

Can I accept this ( )?

INSTANT HAPPINESS – HERE AND NOW

Secret of Happiness
By **Sirshree** Tejparkhi

Copyright © Tejgyan Global Foundation
All Rights Reserved 2011

Tejgyan Global Foundation is a charitable organization
with its headquarters in Pune, India.

ISBN : 978-81-84150-65-0

Published by WOW Publishings Pvt. Ltd., India

First edition: November 2011

Second reprint in December 2022

Printed and bound by Trinity Academy, Pune, INDIA

Copyright and publishing rights are vested exclusively with WOW Publishings Pvt. Ltd. This book is sold subject to the condition that it shall not by way of trade or otherwise, be lent, resold, hired out, or otherwise circulated without the publisher's prior written consent in any form of binding or cover other than that in which it is published and without a similar condition including this condition being imposed on the subsequent purchaser and without limiting the rights under copyright reserved above, no part of this publication may be reproduced, stored in or introduced into a retrieval system, or transmitted, in any form, or by any means, electronic, mechanical, photocopying, recording or otherwise, without the prior written permission of both the copyright owner and the above-mentioned publisher of this book. Any person who does any unauthorized act in relation to this publication may be liable to criminal prosecution and civil claims for damages.

Although the author and publisher have made every effort to ensure accuracy of content in this book, they hereby disclaim any liability to any party for any loss, damage, or disruption caused by errors or omissions, resulting from negligence, accident, or any other cause. Readers are advised to take full responsibility to exercise discretion in understanding and applying the content of this book.

Contents

Preface	5
Chapter 1 Seven Levels of Happiness	7
Chapter 2 Understanding Happiness And Unhappiness	18
Chapter 3 Fulfillment of Desires Is Not The Real Cause of Happiness	22
Chapter 4 Dacoits of Happiness	28
Chapter 5 Let Us Attain Causeless Happiness	36
Chapter 6 First Step To Attain Instant Happiness	42
Chapter 7 Second Step To Attain Instant Happiness	48
Chapter 8 Third Step To Attain Instant Happiness	63
Chapter 9 Learning More About Accepting	65
Chapter 10 Practical Steps for Accepting	71
Chapter 11 Summary	76
Appendices	79

PREFACE

There was a person named Mr. Unhappy. His wife was going to her mother's place for the first time after marriage. She thought, "Before leaving for my home, let me buy something new... like a sari or a dress or something else." Mr. Unhappy gave his consent for it. But then his wife insisted for more and said, "People will appreciate me a lot better at my parent's home if I had a gold necklace." Mr. Unhappy replied, "I don't have that much money, what should I do?" His wife came up with an idea – "I have two gold bangles. Take them with you and get me a beautiful necklace in exchange."

He went to a goldsmith. The goldsmith said, "How can a necklace be made out of just two bangles? It requires a lot of money." "What should I do now?" asked Mr. Unhappy. The goldsmith showed him some imitation necklaces that appeared to be of gold and offered one to Mr. Unhappy saying, "This will solve your purpose." Mr. Unhappy had no choice and so he agreed. Thus with the same money he bought a beautiful, genuine looking necklace. He told the reality to his wife, "It's an artificial necklace. Please make do with this now. I shall buy you a genuine gold one in the future." The wife accepted.

She went to her parents' home wearing a fake necklace. However, there she told everyone that the necklace was a real one as she did not wish to lower her pride. Otherwise how would she feel contented? On her arrival there, her sister-in-law (her brother's wife) saw the necklace and instantly fell in love with it. Now she demanded a necklace from her husband. The husband had to comply although he too did not have enough money to buy it. He went to a goldsmith. The goldsmith told him, "Look, these days imitation jewelry is quite in fashion, why don't you buy it, she may probably like it." Therefore, he too, due to shortage of money, chose one imitation necklace, which was quite similar in appearance. He brought it home and explained to his wife, "Look, although it is an imitation, but right now it will serve your purpose. You will not be envious of my sister's necklace anymore." The wife reluctantly agreed.

One day Mr. Unhappy's wife went for a bath leaving her necklace behind on the dressing table. Seizing the opportunity, her sister-in-law exchanged the necklace with her own. She felt very happy thinking, "Now I have a genuine gold necklace." The second day Mr. Unhappy's wife got an opportunity and she too exchanged the necklace because she had thought that her sister-in-law had a real one. She was pleased with the thought that now she had a gold necklace. Thus, both of them remained in this illusion throughout their lives. Each one thought, "I have a real gold necklace." However, you know that both of them had fake necklaces. They wasted their whole lives acquiring some false happiness.

On listening to this example you feel how foolish they were! However, many people spend all their lives trying to acquire such false happiness. They never find out what real happiness is. Do you also wish for such contentment, which although appears to be true, is actually false? You will see that people all around are completely involved in this kind of fake happiness. But the real bliss, eternal happiness, which is permanent, is always within us. The need does not arise to exchange it for something else because it is genuine. If you find such contentment, then it is bliss, it is real happiness.

CHAPTER 1

SEVEN LEVELS OF HAPPINESS

Everyone desires happiness. Happiness is our true nature. But in our lives happiness is temporary. The quest of spirituality is the quest for permanent happiness, the quest for true happiness – a kind of bliss that does not diminish with time. Man seeks this permanent happiness in his day to day life, but in the process gets entangled in illusory happiness or false happiness.

- False happiness is found in indulging the palate.
- False happiness is what you derive out of winning a lottery.
- False happiness is what you derive when you get a promotion.
- False happiness is found in taunting or even in harming others.
- False happiness is seeking happiness in praise and appreciation.

Transforming the way you derive happiness is the first step in spiritual transformation. There are seven levels of happiness. All the examples of false happiness mentioned above are categorized in the lower levels of happiness. As you spiritually transform, you derive happiness from higher levels.

First level of happiness – Artificial Happiness

Artificial happiness means that where ignorance prevails and where happiness actually does not even exist. Where it does not even occur to one that a fake object is being considered to be an authentic one and our entire life is spent thinking it to be true. What does a person do in this artificial happiness? Let us try to understand it through the examples given below:

1. A person is traveling by bus. He succeeds in making the journey without buying the ticket. Now he is very happy thinking that he has saved Rs. 3, which was the cost of the ticket. This is artificial happiness. It is pointless. Just a little pondering over it would make it clear that there is nothing to be happy about, although at that time it appeared to be real happiness and felt very pleasurable. However, he does not know that due to this false happiness derived from having saved Rs. 3, he perhaps may have created a blockage in money flow in his life amounting to Rs. 300…or Rs. 3000… Rs. 30,000…or maybe even Rs. 300,000.

   This means even a pebble in the pipeline can reduce the flow of water. Money was being generated in our life and happiness was on the cards for us. But because of some blocks or false pleasures, they were not reaching us. Even small pebbles obstruct the flow of water in the water pipe. In order to attain artificial happiness in life, we create blocks; these prevent a lot of things from coming towards us. Those who are not aware of the principles of life keep indulging in artificial happiness due to their ignorance.

2. A man went to watch a movie. He bought a ticket. By mistake, the ticket clerk handed over two tickets instead of

one. Sometimes such mistakes do occur that one may get two tickets instead of one if they are stuck together. Now this man is very pleased that he got two tickets at the price of one. He sells the extra ticket at a higher price and while returning home after watching the movie, he thinks, 'Today I had a great time. I got to watch a movie free, plus I had free snacks… it was wonderful…I enjoyed very much.'

3. A man had taken money on credit from a friend but was not willing to return it. When asked by the friend, "Hey pal! When are you going to return my money?" He replies, "How do I know? Am I a fortune teller that you are asking me?" In this way, many people don't repay their debts.

These are artificial kinds of happiness. If one is using unfair and deceitful means to save money, then it is artificial happiness. Let us move towards genuine happiness without indulging in such things.

Second level of happiness – Second hand happiness

There is a market for second-hand cars where you can buy used cars. However, second-hand vehicles or objects usually don't last long. Similarly, there is second hand happiness, which is derived by using others or having fun at the expense of others. In this type a person likes to enjoy by teasing, taunting, bullying or troubling others. He feels good about it. He likes to make fun of others; it gives him a kind of pleasure. It is just like some friends get together to harass someone and enjoy it. In every school or college, such scenes of ragging are common. This is second hand happiness. Back home you find that brothers and sisters often tease, taunt, and quarrel with each other. And when the dispute grows out of proportion, they patch up by asking for forgiveness from each other, and then throw parties and enjoy themselves. This is the way people nowadays try to find some pleasure and happiness in their lives. When man does not know what is real happiness, he indulges in such kind of happiness.

Whenever we feel happy, we must question ourselves as to what type of happiness it really is.

Third level of happiness – Stimulation Happiness

The third level of happiness is known as stimulation happiness; this happiness is aroused by excitement. For instance a person attending a social gathering or a celebration finds much hustle and bustle happening around. This creates excitement and stimulation. Following are some examples of stimulation happiness :

A) A cricket match is being played and is going to reach the climax...an excitement is created, Oh!! What is going to happen...what will be the final result?...The titillation and anticipation associated with the sport creates a thrill.

B) Some people feel stimulated while watching a suspense movie. Until the secret unfolds, the mind is filled with eagerness and excitement.

C) Happiness gained due to parties, picnics, festivals, celebrations, etc. is stimulation happiness. The whole society today is a prey to this kind of happiness, and it is on the increase day by day. What happens owing to this stimulation and excitement? Suppose now at this time a party is thrown in, and you attend it and return home in a very cheerful mood. You enjoyed thoroughly. But what happens next? On the second day?... On the third day?...Suddenly you find yourself feeling dull and bored. You get bewildered thinking : Why do I feel dull and lifeless on some days? Why do I find myself depressed? Why do I get bored? However, what you don't realize is that what you are feeling today is the result of the party you attended three days back. The body got all excited, all the nerves were tingling, you felt a thrill, you felt alive – "Oh! Something feels new...something feels different..." Then after a few days all that excitement is gone. How do you feel now? Dull…How do you feel now? Burdened…How do you feel now? All alone…lonely…How is this life? Depressing.

The person, who finds out what is the source of boredom, will search for real happiness, he will investigate about it. Those who are completely unaware of real happiness, what will they do? 'Oh! No! Boredom has set in…How can we get back the same enjoyment that we got at the party the other day?' This is what they will think about. So again they will search for a new excitement. "Now what next? What else can I do now?" They will then call up someone and say, "Hey! Let's have a party some day…or let's meet…let's do this…let's do that…" This means no sooner does one excitement get over than the desire for another arises, which creates a new excitement. If there is no such thing, not even a festival, not even a party nor a picnic…then what will they do? Subsequently they will fantasize about such things. You come across many people who keep on fantasizing so as to get stimulated and feel the excitement again. However such gratification is momentary, whether it is due to being in a pub, a gambling den or on a racecourse. As soon as that moment is gone, the same situation continues to persist – of boredom and dullness. A person tries to fight boredom, misery and distress by creating excitement. What he never realizes is, that very excitement in turn leads to even more boredom, misery and distress.

Let us understand this. Whenever excitement is produced in the nervous system, it stimulates the body and makes it energetic. People even tend to get angry many a times because the whole body gets vibrated due to the anger that is generated in the body; and they like it.

For instance when someone scratches himself due to itching, he feels a kind of pleasure as well. But he is not aware that due to scratching, the itch keeps on increasing and the skin disease is worsening. But at that moment he likes it. It is the same with excitement – it feels good when it arises, but as soon as it starts declining, it feels dull, and in the end it feels worse than ever. Then again he will arrange for a party, meet new friends, would wish for something new, so as to feel stimulated and excited again. A higher level of excitement is required the next time around. He may even turn to gambling or some addiction or something else. In this way, his whole life is spent away. He continues to indulge in such kind of pleasures, which has been called as stimulation happiness.

Fourth level of happiness – Formula Happiness

This kind of happiness is created by applying a formula. The meaning of formula is that by combining two things, one formula emerges. Linking two types of pleasures, a formula for happiness is created. When we combine two elements it makes a formula such as $x+y=z$. Students are taught such formulae in schools. Each and every person has devised some formula in his life so as to feel some happiness. If everything goes well as per his formula, he is very happy. For many, the formula is "Sunday morning newspaper + A cigarette + Coffee." For some, the formula is "Saturday night party + A new date every time." For children, the formula could be "A whole day of play + A movie to end the day." For ladies, it could be "Gift + Gold = Happiness."

All these are examples of formula happiness. It does not mean that all this is wrong. However, it reveals the fact that people are not aware of real joy, due to which they indulge in such kind of pleasures.

As you progress further, you will rise above artificial happiness, second hand happiness, stimulation happiness and formula happiness. Then a time will come when you would want to go towards the higher levels. And on approaching the ultimate, what kinds of happiness you will receive has been described below.

Fifth level of Happiness – Happiness through service

This is the first amongst the higher levels of happiness, where an individual derives happiness out of serving others. Some people render service by being instrumental for others in achieving happiness. After recovering from their own maladies and disorders, and after coming out of their own anxieties, they start serving the destitute, the deprived, the aged, and work for the welfare of the society. They get contentment and happiness due to such service.

There are many people who are associated with some voluntary service. They know what immense happiness they attain when they serve others or when they become instrumental for others. However, if the ego does not get dissolved in the process of rendering service, then the service is not achieving its complete objective. 'True service is one in which there is no doer.' It implies that the one who is serving, i.e. the individual ego, the feeling of doership, should dissolve and get eliminated. During the process of service, the dissolving of the ego effectively also results in happiness. This is the happiness that can be attained only through servitude.

The law of nature that states 'Whatever you become a medium for, will multiply in your life' starts paying rich dividends at this level. So, the more one serves, the more happy one becomes, the more Nature rewards him…one really begins to enjoy this virtuous cycle. Many a time, this also leads to bloated egos and high expectations from others. It doesn't take long therefore to fall to the depths of unhappiness from the heights of happiness derived at this level.

Sixth level of Happiness – Divine happiness

At this level of happiness, a person experiences joy due to his devotion to God. Here there is no place for entertainment type of devotion – a lot many things other than worship are being done today in the name of devotion. One such particular occasion is called as *Jaagran* (a religious ceremony carried out in some parts of India). During *Jaagran*, people sing devotional songs and eat and drink throughout the night. And then some people make a pledge : "If this particular desire of ours gets fulfilled, we promise to hold this event at our place next year..." This kind of devotion is either just a kind of entertainment or a business transaction with God. This is the same as is customary in business deals – "You do me a favor, and in return I will do something for you." This type of worship is just a business type of worship; which has got nothing to do with devotion or real happiness. Joy achieved from business type devotion or wavering devotion is not in reality the happiness that is derived through divine veneration. Happiness through worship is gained through intense divine ardour, which is totally different from business or wavering type of devotion. Wavering devotion means the faith that falters when your wishes are not granted by praying to the deities. Consequently, all faith is lost. Then someone advises saying, "There is another deity, let us try that one now." In this way, business devotion is ever persistent. This kind of worship is not at all divine veneration, as there is no awareness of the divine. There is no understanding of what is God. It is just entertainment kind of worship, or devotion that is adulterated with hypocrisy and deceitfulness, or business type of devotion, or wavering faith, or worshipping God for the purpose of atonement. True happiness cannot be derived from such types of devotion. If devotion is done to attain real happiness, only then it is divine devotion.

Happiness acquired from divine devotion is the sixth level of happiness. At this level, man is in love with the Creator. He sings the praises of God and admires everything created by God. Everything that happens in his life is fully acceptable to him. He says, "If God desires to keep me in this state, then I am happy as I am." He believes, "If this is what God desires, then I have no objection to it. If God is making me cry, then I shall cry with happiness..." It is a very beautiful state born out of surrender. There is a level of understanding and spiritual growth out of which this happiness emanates. One is always in a feeling of gratitude and devotion at this level.

Those who know what is divine devotion, they can understand the ultimate happiness. Divine devotion is unconditional. In this type of devotion, our faith, our love for God does not diminish even if our desires are not fulfilled. But if our desire does get fulfilled, then that is a bonus. We are not worshiping in order to get bonus (material gains). We are worshipping for the sake of devotion, for the love of God that has awakened, for the Divinity within, which we have recognized. If divine devotion gets aroused in our hearts, we are bound to get this happiness. Many who are on the path of devotion are working towards it but due to lack of understanding, it results in worshipping blindly, therefore there should not be blind worship. Those who are following the path of devotion should also realize as to what understanding should be combined with it so that their devotion can become divine devotion, and devotion itself should become the ultimate goal. In this kind of veneration, God loves those who love Him. This is the joy of Tej[1] love. This is divine happiness.

Seventh level of happiness – Eternal Bliss

This kind of happiness differs from all other kinds of joys. This happiness is attained when a person is free from all false beliefs and misconceptions, and he knows the answer to, "Who am I?" He attains this happiness after he has realized his true self (self-realization). This happiness arises out of the experience of the Self or the sense of being. It is causeless, unremitting, pure joy that never diminishes and never ends. It is permenant happiness. Each one of us bears the eternal bliss within, but we are not aware of it. Yet everyone does get a glimpse of this joy. When you are in deep sleep and neither the mind is awake nor dreaming, nor are you aware of the body, then you are in connection with that eternal state. So every night when you are in deep sleep, where do you think you are

---

[1] *Tej signifies beyond two, i.e. beyond two polarities. For instance Tej love implies love which is beyond love and hate. Tej Gyan implies knowledge which is beyond knowledge and ignorance. Tej happiness implies happiness which is beyond joys and sorrows.*

- amidst absolute bliss, aren't you? In the morning when you wake up, you say, "I had wonderful sleep." What did you feel in sleep that makes you say so? Where and in which blissful state were you in that deep sleep? And certainly you were in a state of ecstasy. Each and every person in this universe loves going to sleep. Some even take pills in order to get sleep. All the miseries and sorrows, all the aches and pains of the body simply vanish in deep sleep. So what is it that happens during sleep? If we are able to get that 'something' in the wakeful state which happens in deep slumber, then we can get the taste of true happiness.

Every child until the age of 2½ years (before the contrast mind begins to develop) is established in the above mentioned state of awareness, in the experience of the Self, in eternal bliss. He sees every joy from that state. As soon as the child grows older, his contrast mind begins to develop. Contrast mind is distinct from the simple or instinctive mind. It signifies that mind which judges, compares, evaluates and splits everything into two – black or white. Just as there is a contrast control system in television, similarly a mind is formed within us which discriminates between black and white. After seeing anything, it says – this is good, that is bad. For instance, when you are listening to someone or watching or reading something, a commentary is always going on in your mind – "This that has been said is good…this wasn't anything special…well I already know this…" In this way some or the other commentary is constantly on in the mind. This is known as the contrast mind. Until and unless it attains understanding, it cannot sit quiet.

Today people are agonized due to their thoughts, due to their minds. If a thought arises, it refuses to budge. The same thought recurs again and again; the same stress, the same pressure continues – "Oh no! Am I going to fail?…Oh! What will happen if I do not get a promotion?…What will happen tomorrow?…What should I do about this thing?…If guests arrive now, what will I do?…. How will

I complete all the tasks? So many thoughts rush in all at once and no brakes can be applied to them. And we can see that it is thoughts that lead to misery; and it keeps on increasing. Hence the contrast mind needs training. If this contrast mind gets training to become a child again, then the same mind will be the cause for happiness.

■

CHAPTER 2

UNDERSTANDING HAPPINESS AND UNHAPPINESS

Training to become a child again

Every child remains in the experience of the true Self (absolute bliss) till the age of 2½ years. If you have a child at home, observe him closely. If you don't have any kids at home, you can observe the children in your neighborhood. Observe as to how they see things – they see a body opposite to them, but they are totally unaware that they too have a body. They feel that only other people have a body, they don't feel that they themselves also have a body.

You show a toy rattle to an infant in a cradle. And showing him toys, he is being trained that "Come out of your experience of Self; come out of that bliss. Become fit to live in our community, in our society. Otherwise if you remain in that state, you will be useless, you will be no good." It is in this society that we have to raise that child. So it is necessary to bring him out from that state. But he never again gets the chance to return within. In this situation, that child becomes old even before he grows up.

But now the time has come – to become a child again, to return to that experience of the Self, that sense of being, that eternal bliss. That experience which every child experiences, even you have experienced it. No one can say that I was never a child. Every person was initially a child and was in that experience. There the experience was 'There is a body opposite to me, but on my side there is no body.' He is watching everything from a state of witnessing, there is nothing other than that. Then gradually he becomes aware that he has a body. People tell him, "This body is you." And then he forgets his real state, the Self experience, the eternal bliss.

Hence if you want to experience your true self, you have to become a child again. In Tej Gyan Foundation, you are given training to become a child. On reading this, no one should jump to the conclusion that here they make us a child again, that means we will have to begin babbling like a child. It is not so. One has to get stabilized in that experience of the Self, that sense of being, which the child experiences. And being in that state, you will take all your decisions. If we are not in that experience of life, our decisions are that of an individual (involving ego, fear, greed, hatred, jealousy, etc.). Decisions are taken by believing ourself to be a separate entity, i.e. separate from all other people.

An exercise to understand our own self

Observe your hands for a minute. Ask yourself : Am I this hand? Answer this from your feeling right now. How do you relate yourself with your hand? Observe intently what you feel. Here two types of feelings may arise. Some people may feel, "Yes, I am this hand" and others may answer, "I am not this hand."

Those whose answer is "I am this hand" should think: "If this hand is cut, then will I be no more? Or will I cease to exist? Is that so?" The answer is no, it is not so. Even if your hands are cut off, yet you are there and you are complete. The feeling within you, the experience says, **"I am complete."** For example, in an accident if someone loses his limbs, he still says, "I am complete." He never says, "I was complete earlier and now I am incomplete." Because when the body is cut, *you* do not get cut. When you start experiencing this truth, then you will understand. For this, you will first have to understand through the intellect as to what you are not. Then you will have to understand "Who are you?" You will have to understand this in a step-by-step manner. (Perform the same exercise with each part of the body as to whether I am this eye… am I these feet… am I this skin… am I this face…). Instant happiness is attained as soon as you come to know who you really are.

Cause of unhappiness – false beliefs and misconceptions

Many false beliefs and misconceptions are deeply ingrained in your minds. It is due to these beliefs that troublesome thoughts keep recurring in your mind. Some people believe that if a cat crosses the road, it is a bad omen for the one who goes further. But does it actually happen or is it just a belief? You should ask yourselves seriously as to what happens if a cat crosses the road? Some believe that they will receive plenty of money if they get an itching sensation in the palms of their hands. Let us ponder seriously over such beliefs – does it really happen or is it just a notion? Because when these beliefs came into existence, the circumstances, the environment and the people were different from today. At that time electricity had not been discovered yet. Also in those days, different communities had different beliefs. In a certain community the date 13 is considered as very unlucky, hence all people in that community believe the date 13 to be ill-fated and do everything fearfully on that date. But just come to think of it, is it true that the date 13 is ominous or is it only one of our erroneous beliefs? Some believe that fluttering of eyes, wearing black clothes, or breaking of a mirror is inauspicious. Some also believe that if someone has a haircut or his beard trimmed on a particular day, then something bad will happen to him. There are many such beliefs that you must have heard of. So, is there any truth in them or are they just your beliefs? In fact, these are all just the suppositions and superstitions of the mind. These are just a few of them that were brought to light but the whole world is full of beliefs and misconceptions. Each person must be having a different set of beliefs, due to which he attracts a lot of trouble, unhappiness and suffering in his life. People do not even know that they have become withdrawn and closed due to these mistaken beliefs.

Everything in our life is related to beliefs and the way you have been brought up to see those beliefs. Your fears, your sorrows, your joys, your successes, your failures, your life, your death... everything is based on your beliefs. Beliefs are something that you believe in, but are actually not true. Some beliefs have been devised by people to suit their conveniences, but you laugh and cry according to them. In fact, you lead your entire life according to them. We need to come out of these beliefs.

Why are we not getting happiness? We have to find the actual reason for this. Our happiness lies within ourselves. We don't need to go to a theatre or an amusement park for that. We don't need to wait for any promotion or for a party. We just need to search for it. In spite of having happiness within ourselves, we are not feeling it. The reason is we have become withdrawn and closed. If we open up, only then will that happiness manifest. Therefore, we need to find out the cause behind mankind becoming withdrawn and closed. After knowing that, we have to understand how to get instant happiness. We are going to understand this subject step by step. Up till now we have understood the cause of unhappiness and the seven levels of happiness. The secret of real happiness was revealed as the seventh kind of happiness. We will understand this in more detail through an analogy in the next chapter.

■

CHAPTER 3

FULFILLMENT OF DESIRES IS NOT THE REAL CAUSE OF HAPPINESS

The Greatest Misunderstanding

Man lives under the illusion that happiness is obtained by fulfillment of desires. But let us understand the hidden missing link behind it. In order to illustrate this clearly, four pictures have been displayed.

1)   In the first picture, there is a person standing in front of a wall and on the other side of the wall, there is a light. You may call it God or Light of Truth, some may call it Allah, Truth, Lord, or Self – different names have been given by different people. It is the real source of all happiness.

This wall is the 'Wall of Desires'. The person in the picture is *you*. After looking at it do not think, "My face is not like this…I am a woman, this picture is of a man." This picture is a depiction of you; in fact it is a depiction of all of us.

In this picture, a wall is built with the many desires of man. Each desire denotes a stone block in the wall. Someone wants a car, someone desires a ranch, someone wants status or a job or a promotion, and so on. Whatever the desires, all are written on the

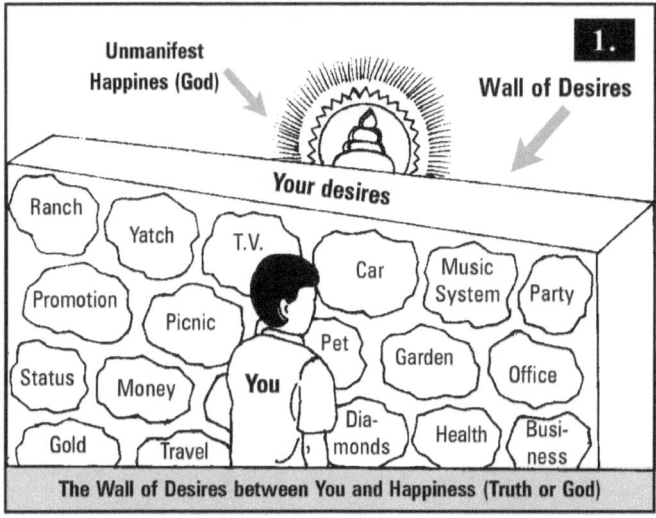

The Wall of Desires between You and Happiness (Truth or God)

stone blocks. And there is something at the back of the wall, which has got covered and hidden, that which is within us. It merely needs to be revealed, it needs to be uncovered. Only after attaining it and realizing it, can we attain real happiness.

2) In the next picture you can see that a person is continuously repeating in his mind just like chanting a mantra on a rosary – I want a car...I want a car...I wish I have a car...I want to have a car...I want a promotion...I want a promotion...I want a pet...I want a pet....and he keeps on counting the beads repeatedly. The mind is filled up with those desires. Then suddenly one day he gets a car, a promotion, or a pet – whatever he desired. As soon as he got it, the block of that desire disappeared, and as you see in the second picture – the God hidden behind is seen, i.e. real happiness manifests. You saw a small part of it, a little glimpse, and you felt happy. But this was misinterpreted and you thought that you felt happy because you got the object of your desire. Man falls a victim to this great misunderstanding that happiness results from the fulfillment of desires. And then he spends his entire life in the pursuit of fulfillment of his desires. In the process, he has acquired

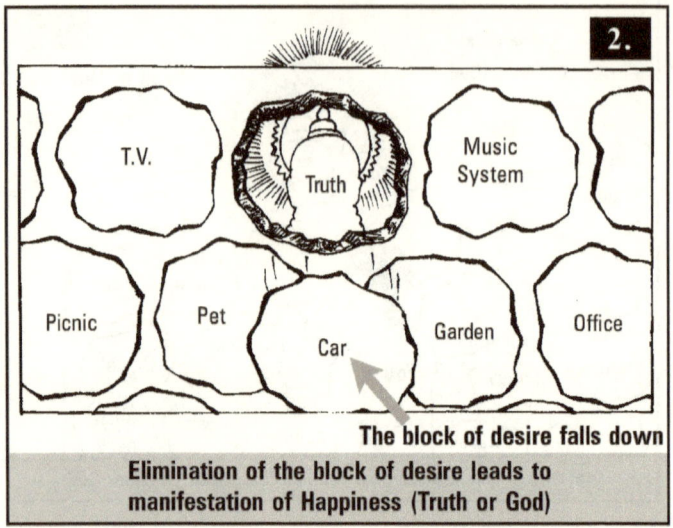

The block of desire falls down
Elimination of the block of desire leads to manifestation of Happiness (Truth or God)

the habit of craving for desires. Now there cannot be a greater loss than this. This is similar to the one who has the habit of scratching himself : even without any itching he will keep on scratching and worsening the disease. In the same way one gets habituated to having desires. It becomes an obsessive compulsion for him. Even if all wishes of man are fulfilled, still he will think, 'Now what else should I have?' He will just not be able to sit quiet without any desires. He will try to awaken new desires and in this manner this cycle will continue. He is never able to understand that the mind, which was filled with a desire, suddenly got emptied because that desire was fulfilled. And in that emptiness, in that 'nothingness', in that state of 'no mind' – real happiness manifested. 'No mind' signifies the state when there is no mind or the mind is blank, i.e. there are no desires, no thoughts, nothing. The meaning of mind is a sack or bundle of all the desires put together. That is the mind. The accumulation of all thoughts and all desires is mind.

Thus, the mind is full of desires. One desire of it gets fulfilled and happiness (God) manifests. Whatever may be the definition of God for you, it may differ for different people, but we shouldn't get stuck with words and assume that this is being told for the Hindus. Here we are not speaking about Hindus, Muslims, Sikhs, Christians or Jews, but the *real happiness, which is within all of us.*

Each person desires real happiness. Whatever you do, ask yourself the question, "Why am I doing this?" Initially the answers will be, "I am doing this for the sake of my friend or I am doing it for my family." Then think about it further: "If my family becomes happy then what will happen?" – "I will feel relaxed, I will feel content, then I will get happiness." You will see that finally the answer will be : "I will get happiness."

The intention behind everything we do is contentment and real happiness. This is the only thing that each and every one desires, but does not know how to get it. Therefore we have to understand this secret.

3) You can see in the third picture that one more desire has awakened – "I want a house." This desire has taken the place of the earlier desire for a car. Now because of this desire, once again the

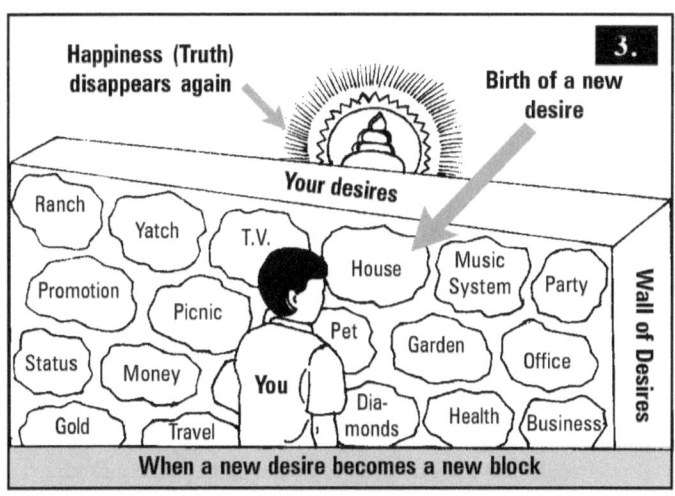

happiness gets obscured. Subsequently again some desire will get fulfilled, once more happiness (God) will come into sight. Thus after fulfillment of each desire, happiness arises because of attainment of the real thing (Truth, Self, God). This is the secret that you should know. Until now no matter how many joys you have received, they have all been due to the manifestation of the Truth, and not due to achieving something or fulfillment of any desire. Each and every joy is attained due to the Truth that manifests from within. After you get this understanding, you will be able to see God and experience the bliss whenever you like.

4) In the last picture you will see that all the stone blocks of desires have disappeared and real happiness (God) is fully manifest. Here a picture depicting God is shown; it is just symbolic. People imagine about the appearance of God – we have two hands, so he may be having four. Those who had attained self-realization had created idols of God in order to make the masses understand. So that people should be able to prostrate before the idols and surrender, and get rid of the mind, and achieve a state of 'no mind'. Idols were created

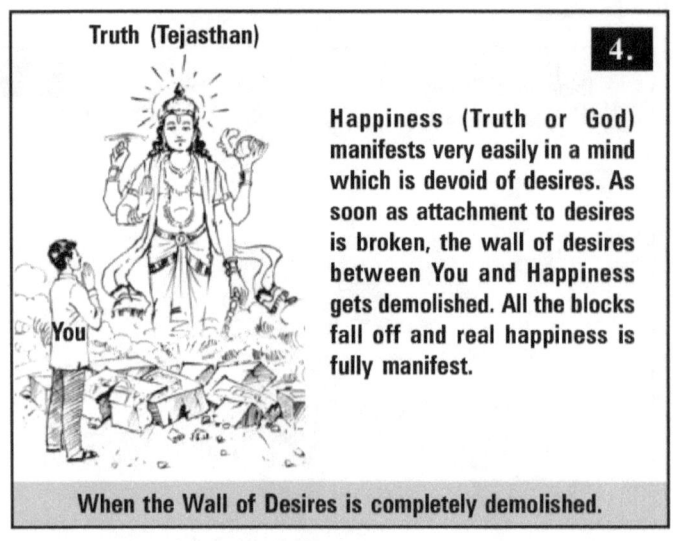

When the Wall of Desires is completely demolished.

for helping us, but instead there is violence and bloodshed in the name of temples and mosques (between those who worship idols and those who don't).

Those who had built temples, mosques or churches had a higher objective in mind. Today the real meaning of it is lost. By going to a temple, mosque or a church, we had to learn about how to get the state of 'no mind', how to attain liberation from the Wall of Desires. We have forgotten that motive today. Therefore to attain the seventh type of happiness, we have to think about : How to demolish this wall? How to attain that inner experience, that sense of being, that absolute bliss which we experienced as a child? The state that was experienced in deep sleep, how to achieve the same experience in the wakeful state? How energetic and how fresh you feel after sleep! You will be transformed if you are able to achieve the experience that you get during deep sleep in your wakeful state. You will be amazed to find that there is so much power within you that you were not even aware of. It was just that the mind had consumed all that energy, which can now be saved by staying in the state of experience of Self, and all the tasks will be dealt with easily.

■

CHAPTER 4

DACOITS OF HAPPINESS

Beware of the dacoits within you

As soon as you open your eyes in the morning, what kind of thought enters your mind? You see a body opposite you. 'I am a body and the opposite person is also a body' – this misconception enters the mind. The beginning itself is made with false beliefs. You believe yourself to be a body and live a fearful, restricted and closed life. Tendencies are formed due to beliefs. A belief goes in the mind and a tendency is formed and that becomes a habit. For example, the moment you wake up, thoughts start arising within you… Now I have to do this…now I have to do that…today I have to complete this project…I have to prepare breakfast…I have to get my children ready for school…So many thoughts come rushing in, due to which tendencies or patterns are formed. What happens due to these tendencies, let us understand this through the following example.

The moment you open your eyes in the morning, thoughts rush in. This has been likened to dacoits invading the mind. And you know very well what happens when the dacoits rush in, you may have seen such type of scenes in movies. In movies you see scenes of a carnival and then the dacoits come rushing in on horses. The next scene shows that the dacoits have left and the scene of the carnival is shown again in which you see that the assailants have destroyed everything and have left. It is exactly the same thing that happens with you. In the morning no sooner you open your eyes than the dacoits of thoughts force their way in and destroy everything within you and leave. Consequently, the repair work continues throughout the day to put back together everything that had been damaged by the dacoits of thoughts in the morning. So, when will you attain real happiness?

Why don't we have any control over these dacoits of thoughts? Why do these dacoits come in? What is it within you that invites them? Let us understand this. There is an informer or a spy (mind) within you. This informer sends out information. As you must be knowing there is such a person in the Police Department who is planted by the enemy. He divulges all information and all plans to the opponent. All information is passed on to the enemy. As soon as you open the window (eyes), all the horses (thoughts) rush in. And then those thoughts create misery, and with that misery a person gets down from the bed. He perhaps may have listened to K.G. (kindergarten) kind of spiritualism. There are so many types of 'spiritual' activities happening around, where using some fear or some enticement, people are taught, "You should carry out your actions in this particular manner. What is happening with you now is the result of your deeds in your previous birth. Now if you perform these specific actions in this birth, then these actions will bear fruit in your next life. Nothing substantial is going to happen in this birth, you will have to take seven more births, only then will you attain liberation. Your salvation is not possible in this life. If you perform these many deeds, then you will be saved from the agony of seven more rebirths. And if you perform this particular ritual, then you will be spared from one more birth..." This is the kindergarten spiritual knowledge that is being wrongly taught to all. They will even tell you to put your right foot down first as you get off from the bed in the morning so that you can have a nice day ahead.

Perhaps you have risen above your false beliefs but if you still believe that "I am this body. All these tasks are *my* responsibilities. I am the doer. Nothing can be accomplished without me. The world does not function without me. If I won't go to this place now, everything will come to a standstill." With all such kinds of beliefs, even if you put forth the right foot while alighting from the bed, it will be as good as the left (wrong) one. But as soon as you open your eyes and ask yourself, "Who am I?" and with this understanding of your true self even if you put forth your left foot first, yet it will be right (correct). Therefore, on opening your eyes in the morning, observe how is your state of mind. If a lot of thoughts are entering your mind, then what should you do? Understand this through an example:

In the morning after opening your eyes, you open the doors and windows of your house. As soon as the window is opened, a storm comes rushing in. But if you already know that there is a storm outside, then you place all objects in the house appropriately before opening the window. Initially you arrange your possessions in a certain manner to protect them. Then you open the window a little to check the force of the storm. If it is okay, only then you fully open the window. In the same way when we open our eyes in the morning, what do we do? We open the window of our eyes, don't we? But before opening the window, wait for a little while, and tell yourself, "Now I am going to open the window, and these specific kinds of beliefs will come rushing in and will trouble me a lot, such as : Today is a bad day…today is not such a good day… today those new guests are going to arrive… today I have do this…" All distressing thoughts start arising. At that time you should tell those thoughts: "Stop!" And before opening your eyes ask yourself, "How do I want to start my day? How do I want to live today's day?

What do I have to accept today? What kind of miracles do I want to expect? How are my thoughts? Are they happy thoughts or not? Am I going to start my day with negative thoughts today?" In this way you should prepare yourself from within and only then begin the day. This is how you will be putting your best foot forward while alighting from the bed. Then you will find only miracles happening in your life. Then you will open your window (eyes) in the right direction (with understanding). Then there won't be any storm because you have opened the window in the right direction.

Awakening in truth

So when we open our eyes, in which direction should we open our eyes? It is very important to know this. Because we can direct our body and mind the way we want to. We had first opened our window towards *Maya* (the world of illusion), now we can open it towards the Truth – just the direction is changed. Change of direction in this way can lead to a miracle. Then thoughts of nothing but the Truth will arise from you.

Now from today onwards when we open our eyes in the morning, our awakening shall be in Truth (sense of being) because during the entire night we were with that Truth. We were with the God that was present behind the wall, which you have seen in the picture. It is explained with the help of pictures. You have to be transformed into a child again. You have been shown some pictures and some new pictures have to be shown to you. When you were being taught alphabets in school, you have seen and learnt many pictures, i.e. A for Apple, B for Bat… But now a new era has set in, now the time has come to see Truth in the right perspective. We have to come out of *our idea* of the Truth, it's time to leave such imaginations aside and come out of it. Then while alighting down from the bed whichever foot you put down, it will be with the understanding of "*Who* has put the foot down?"

Get rid of patterns

Whichever thoughts arise in our minds, have we ever questioned ourselves that these thoughts that crop up within me, why don't they arise in my friend's mind? The thoughts that arise within you, do not arise within your friend's mind, because you have a different set of beliefs as compared to him. All the incidents that have occurred with you since your childhood are different from his. You have become closed and withdrawn due to those experiences, and that too in your own way. We have to work on ourselves. We have to ask ourself, "What should I do so that the window opens in the right direction? Which are the patterns that I have to get rid off so that I can become more open?" Patterns mean the tendencies and habits. These too are the dacoits of our happiness. Some patterns have been described below:

1. **Fire pattern** : Those who possess the fire pattern scream and shout over every little thing. Even if such people speak softly, still it feels like they are shouting. People of fire pattern respond to each and every situation with anger and rage. In fact this becomes their habit. How will the thoughts of Truth arise in such a person? Thoughts of Truth will not arise as long as there is an informer, a spy – the mind – present within that invites such thoughts. If that informer stops working, thoughts of fire pattern will also cease.

2. **Fear pattern** : Those who possess the fear pattern always live in fear and are therefore always withdrawn and closed. Wherever they go, they have this fear that someone is watching them, and hence they become withdrawn and closed. Even if these people want to tell something about themselves, they are unable to talk and communicate with others. They are just not able to speak. They can never ask anything from others. This is Fear pattern.

3. **Liar Pattern** : Those who possess the liar pattern are very deceitful. Such people lie in every situation. They have the habit of speaking lies. Even when there is absolutely no necessity to lie, yet they resort to lying. This is Liar Pattern, a pattern of deceit.

4. **Blamer Pattern** : If you say anything to people having the blamer pattern, they will say, "He did this, therefore this has happened... she has done this, so that has occurred... it is because of rain today that this has taken place... today it is chilly, hence this has happened... someone else is responsible for my unhappiness... somebody is doing something, that is why I am unhappy." If you ask, "Why haven't you done this work?" They will immediately reply, "What happened is ... and that is why... he..." No sooner do these people get an excuse than they stop working. They sit to study, there is a power failure. Now they have an excuse. Any excuse is enough to deter them from working on anything. These people always blame others for everything they do or don't do.

5. **Breaker Pattern** : Those who possess the breaker pattern do begin a task, but leave it incomplete. Most of their tasks are left in the lurch.

6. **Blaster Pattern** : Some people have a blaster pattern. Supposing someone is going on talking something nasty and this person is bearing everything calmly. For months together, he does not react to it, he goes on suppressing all his anger within. Then one fine day, he explodes. He screams, shouts, says many a spiteful things, creates a havoc, throws objects and destroys everything. This type of a pattern has been called as a Blaster Pattern.

7. **Miser Pattern** : Some people have a miser pattern, i.e. they are miserly or stingy. They are tightfisted about everything. Even when they laugh, they do it sparingly. If someone tells

them a joke, these people will laugh in a miserly way; they think that they will go home and then laugh a little bit more. They have become closed due to this pattern. They do not know what their possibilities are. We have attained a human body, so what are the unlimited possibilities that we have? And what has happened due to this miserliness? Stinginess that is exercised in money matters also extends to each and every aspect of life. Even if they want to become happy, they raise a doubt on happiness thinking, "It is temporary, so why be happy at all? This reason for happiness will end, so why should we feel happy? Okay, there is something to laugh about; but then why laugh so much?" They won't laugh. But when these people open up, it is only then that they realize, "Oh! We were losing out on such tremendous joy. We were getting such a great opportunity to become a child again and we were losing it."

8. **Timer Pattern** : Some people have the timer pattern. These people never reach anywhere on time. They start from home at the right time but do not reach their destination on time. Even if they start an hour or even two hours earlier, they will come across someone on the way, or something or the other will happen, due to which they will be late. Because of this they have developed the pattern of always being late.

Patterns signify predisposition, tendencies, habits, inclinations – things that we do repeatedly and compulsively, sometimes consciously and sometimes unconsciously. Many a time we know our patterns and do not like them, but we still repeat them because we have become programmed for them. Some examples of patterns have been explained above. Because of patterns many a people have become slaves of their destinies. The lines of their palms show what will happen in their future. These people live life mechanically.

Whatever the lines of their hands indicate, the same happens with them.

Who is the real fortunate one

What do the lines on the palms indicate? They indicate the tendencies, habits, patterns – this person belongs to this type of pattern, so this is what is definitely going to happen with him, this is his destiny. But when he opens up, when he attains wisdom, it is then that he rises above his lines. **The real fortunate is the one who gets liberation from his destiny.** Attaining liberation from one's destiny is opening up a great possibility; and this possibility is present in all of us. But unless we get rid of our patterns, our false beliefs and preconceived ideologies, we will never be able to fully open up and blossom. A belief is just a thought; a thought such as: "People are bad," "The world has gone to the dogs," "I shall always remain a failure," "Resources are scarce, so I shouldn't give anything to others…" We are living with many such kinds of thoughts, but God has created everything in abundance. There is no dearth of anything, everything is abundant. However, when man began to accumulate due to his greed, consequently it became less for some people. If each and every person of the universe became open and honest, then there will never be a dearth of anything – neither food, nor money or anything else. Therefore let us get rid of these patterns and beliefs, cast aside our closed and withdrawn existence, and live openly and fully.

■

CHAPTER 5

LET US ATTAIN CAUSELESS HAPPINESS

Man, due to his fear and feeling of insecurity, keeps on creating blocks. He creates a borderline that this is my country and that is yours, this is my home and that is yours, this is my body and that is yours. He becomes closed and stops opening up. Now the time has come to open up. We should open up and see what happiness we have within us. For that purpose we will perform an exercise.

Close your eyes for a minute and recall any one occasion of happiness that had occurred in your life. See in your mind one such moment when you were extremely happy. Bring to your mind such a picture and recall the feelings of that joyous moment. Whichever cherished ecstatic moment you have in your life, feel its ecstasy. Do this exercise for a few moments and then open your eyes. Now the question is that you felt happy, but was there any reason behind it? Had any such event occurred due to which you had felt happy?

Different answers can be given to this question but the fact is that you had not felt happy without a reason. There was some reason that had made you happy. Now just eliminate that reason, whatever it was – you had won a lottery, you had received a promotion, you had met someone who made you feel very happy... Just remove the reason or cause. That happiness which you felt, if you can get the same happiness without any cause, how will that be? If you can attain that same joy whenever you want and that too without any reason, then how will your life be? That is what is being tried to convey to you – about how to attain happiness without a reason. Because if you want to attain happiness which is due to some reason then that happiness will not be permanent. That will be temporary happiness, which is dependent on a cause or reason. If you want to attain instant happiness then you will have to understand how we receive happiness without a cause.

Our sense of being is enough to attain happiness. Just your being is sufficient to make you feel blissful. How many people have you met till date who say that "I am" and so I am happy. Our beingness is sufficient, we are alive, this is more than enough. A person, who is on the verge of death and is gasping for breath, becomes aware at that time that he was living and he was breathing. Otherwise no one is aware that they are alive. *We are alive*, this is such a great cause for happiness, but our beliefs do not allow us to be happy. Our beliefs tell us, "So what? We are all alive." But what is the meaning of being alive? What is it due to which this body is seen to be moving about? What is it due to which this body is seen to be talking and singing? What is it within the nightingale that makes it sing? What is it that has occurred inside it? Hasn't that occurred with us too? The same has happened with us too, but why don't we sing songs? What kind of thoughts, what kind of dacoits have entered in our minds? What kind of informers are working inside us that are preventing us from being happy? Something like that has definitely happened. We have to understand this thing. All the exercises or experiments that you did were to enable you to understand how to attain true happiness, permanent happiness, eternal happiness.

The first and foremost requirement of the world – to blossom, to open up, to attain instant happiness

There are three types of people in the world – the closed, the stuck and the open. Tej Gyan Foundation is engaged in helping all types of people to open up and blossom.

1. **The closed** : The closed are those who become withdrawn and closed at every opportunity in life. When you have a cold water bath, your body recoils and withdraws. Likewise the closed are those who withdraw within themselves when people laugh at them. They close when their self-image is hurt. Or when somebody doesn't do what they wanted them to do. Or when they have unwanted guests at home. All they do is to snivel, shudder and shrink. They withdraw and resist everything – big and small. These are different examples that illustrate how they become withdrawn and closed due to fear and insecurity. They feel that by becoming closed they are defending themselves but they don't know that they are getting into a wrong habit. When they realize (if they realize) the secret of life is all about blossoming, life becomes magical for them. They are amazed at the life they were living so far. They wonder, how could they have survived for so long? Were they even living? They realize that having been bereft of this simple secret, every moment of theirs was filled with fear and worry. For the closed, understanding the secret of blossoming is incredible and magical.

2. **The stuck** : These are the kind of people who are stuck somewhere or the other. They are entangled and caught up in their little mental blocks, in their own small worlds and always feel suppressed. They are better than the closed. At least, they don't withdraw further. But they are caught up at one place, not growing and no more opening up. Many opportunities come their way, but they are so stuck with their problems and way of living, that it is to no avail. They may have overcome big challenges, but get stuck in something extremely

insignificant. Some are stuck with the idea of revenge. Some with the misconception that they have been wronged. They just seethe and remain stuck. When the stuck realize the secret that life is all about blossoming, they come unstuck and their energy is released. Realizing the secret brushes and touches them up. It is like they have found a broom to clean all the filth within and the filth that they consistently observe in others. Their webs of illusion, false beliefs and myths of life are instantly cleared.

3. **The open** : These people are already open – open to growth. Just a little push and they start to blossom. For them realizing the secret of blossoming works like a helicopter. It shows them a helicopter view of life, i.e. seeing from the perspective of a helicopter. Say you are in Delhi and are confused by its roads. You cannot make out where do all those lanes emerge from and where do they lead to. But when you view this picture from above, from the helicopter, you find that the whole picture is revealed, i.e. at once all the roads are visible. In this way Tejgyan makes you see from the perspective of the helicopter. When the people who are open realize and imbibe the secret of blossoming in their life, they take off with utmost clarity and foresight.

What is this secret of blossoming all about? It is simple. All it says is that every opportunity in life is there only for you to blossom. Every incident occurs to test you and to see if you blossom or not. Look at children and animals. Do they become closed at every opportunity? They live naturally and operate out of their being. They operate from nothingness and are open. They intuitively know that the secret of life is blossoming. But as they grow up they start to withdraw and become closed. A time comes when they completely withdraw into a shell. Their hearts become cold and closed. The earlier they realize the secret, the better it is to return to a childlike (not childish) way of living and looking at life.

Let's do a small exercise to understand what blossoming is all about and also to enable you to feel the joy of opening up and letting go of all inhibitions.

Hands Opening Experiment

Right now, at this instant, keep this book aside and perform the following exercise because we want to enjoy the process of opening up. Check yourself. How is your posture? If you feel that it is stressed, change it, and relax. Open both your hands. Spread out both your arms in the direction of the sky with open hands. Tell yourself that you are open to receive all the blossoming that life offers to you. Feel the happiness, the pleasure of blooming. Be in this posture for 30 seconds. Now put your hands down.

After doing this exercise, contemplate on the following:

1. Did you feel good while performing this exercise?
2. Did you feel open?
3. By performing this exercise, were you able to feel yourself free from that withdrawn and closed feeling? Or did you experience a strange feeling inside you?
4. If you are asked to do the same exercise amidst a hundred people, what would you feel? Would you hesitate to do so in front of everybody? Or would you feel weird? Whatever is your feeling, experience it.

Many a time we feel hesitant and scared to carry out such experiments. We feel that if there are six hundred people around us, that means twelve hundred eyes are watching 'me', we feel scared and withdraw. Because it is our tendency that whenever someone is watching us, we become withdrawn and closed. We have never lived freely, we have never walked freely. When we will find out what it is to bloom, it's only then that real happiness will be manifested due to opening up. Therefore start this experiment from today itself. If you want to attain happiness then you will have to break through this closedness.

And of course, while doing this exercise make use of your common sense as to where you should do this experiment. Select surroundings that are suitable and comfortable for you to perform this experiment. When you are alone, then spread out your hands. You can do this exercise on the terrace or in the park too. Check yourselves intermittently as to how you are sitting – whether you are sitting openly or are you all cringed up? If you feel that you are cringed up, then relax yourself and sit comfortably. If we are living timidly, this has to stop, it is time to open up and blossom. Then we will feel the happiness that comes with blossoming. We cannot increase the size of our body much, but through our mind we can expand over the entire universe. We can enlarge our mind as much as we want. We flourish in joy, we withdraw in sorrow. From this withdrawn and closed state, we have to reach the state of expansion, and the distance between the two has to be covered. Otherwise the entire lives of some people are spent in this interval.

■

CHAPTER 6

FIRST STEP TO ATTAIN INSTANT HAPPINESS

'Can I accept this?'

This is a small but very powerful mantra or maxim which you have to repeat in order to attain instant happiness. Whenever you find yourself withdrawn and closed, repeat this mantra. In life we come across many unwanted situations that in turn lead to misery. Even trivial incidents make us retreat in our shell and make us very unhappy. To come out of that unhappiness, we have to make use of this mantra. The mantra is, 'Can I accept this?' While asking yourself this question, create the symbol of a bracket such as ( ) using the thumb and index finger of your right hand. 'Can I accept this?' Here 'this' implies what is happening at this particular moment, at present. Put in the bracket ( ) that what is affecting you from outside or from within you. For instance, some unfavorable incident has occurred or you are feeling depressed, then just ask yourself, "Can I accept this?" ('This' means that unfavorable incident or your depression).

Let us understand it in detail through some more examples. (Whenever you repeat this mantra, make a shape of a bracket with the help of your thumb and your forefinger as shown in the picture of the hand. This small sign will immediately transfer you into a feeling of acceptance).

1. You are waiting for the lift. It is taking a long time. Now you are feeling a little irritated about this. So ask yourself, "Can I accept this?" The answer will emerge, "Why not? Yes, I can accept it." This will relax you instantly. The stress which was present in the body will get released at once. Just because we do not know this mantra, we continue to become withdrawn, closed and stressed frequently.

2. You are making a phone call to someone. You can hear the bell ringing at the other end, but nobody is picking it up. You are getting impatient – "Come on, pick it up, pick it up quickly." At that moment, just ask yourself, "Can I accept this?" The answer will come from within you, "Yes, I can accept it." Now you can listen to the phone bell ringing comfortably.

3. There are many such small things that irritate and trouble the mind. For instance, something falling down or even the breaking of a plate causes distress. At that time just repeat this mantra, 'Can I accept this ( )?' Put 'breaking of the plate' in the bracket, i.e. "Can I accept the breaking of the plate?" "I can accept it." If a thought of fear has arisen in your mind, then put 'thought of fear arising' in the bracket. Whatever is happening at that moment, repeat the mantra, 'Can I accept this ( )?'

In this way when we accept a situation, our power to tackle that situation is enhanced to a great degree. 'Can I accept this?' – this little mantra can work wonders. Whenever any situation arises, you will find that the answer will be 'yes' 100% in smaller incidents. It is only because we haven't asked ourself that we have become withdrawn and closed. Now after repeating this mantra, you won't live a closed life anymore.

When you will get the benefit of this mantra in smaller incidents, you will find that in 99% of the average occurrences also the answer will be 'yes'. Examples of average or medium occurrences are a small accident or someone insulting you, in which case you flinch back instantly. At that moment ask yourself, 'He has insulted me, can I accept this?' You will see that in 99% of the cases, your answer will be 'yes'. With this you will be immediately freed from that thought. After the answer 'yes', many of your problems will be solved. Just make a habit of asking yourself in every situation, 'Can I accept this?' Then it may so happen that your neighbour's dog will not allow you to sleep with its incessant barking, something may go wrong as soon as you wake up in the morning, someone may do some mischief, or you may hear the blaring of a music system. In any case, just ask yourself, "Can I accept this?" And if you are able to accept that noise then you will say, "Let it go on. If the dogs are barking, let them bark, I am accepting it." With this acceptance, the stress that was in the process of being built up within you will immediately get released and a feeling of relief will instantly flood through you. You can of course take corrective action after that, which will be more composed and effective.

If you are told that for two hours you are not going to budge from here, then repeating the mantra 'Can I accept this?' will relax you at once and you will be able to sit with ease. When you have accepted the situation, then you can sit comfortably. Now there is no hurry at all, no need to constantly look at the watch or the cell phone, because you have accepted. As soon as you accept any situation, you instantly feel happiness that arises due to acceptance. The mantra 'Can I accept this?' covers the gap between being closed and expansion. This will create miracles in your life.

With this mantra if the answer comes "No, I cannot accept this", then you should accept the non-acceptance as well. You will be able to understand this through an example. If you feel, "I can't tolerate this man's face," then ask yourself, "Can I accept my unacceptability?" If you are worried and that worry is constantly eating you, just ask yourself, "Can I accept this worry?" Your answer will be, "Alright, so I am worried. I can accept it." In this way when you accept your unacceptability, something new is created. When you accept your non-acceptance that "Okay. This is the way I am, I have faults, but this is fine by me, I accept it," you will be amazed by the results of this acceptance. A person who is fat or short is unable to accept himself. Someone says, "I have ugly teeth, I cannot accept this." But with this mantra he will say, "Alright, I can accept this unacceptability."

It is possible that you get a negative answer in some situation. In that case, give yourself some time, and after an interval, ask again. For instance, some incident has occurred and you are unable to accept it. You feel it is not acceptable and your answer is 'no'. So say "Fine. I am not accepting it." After some time ask again, "Can I accept this now?" And you will find that after some time a positive answer will start emerging. This is likely in some instances. A positive answer may not come immediately, but after a few minutes or a few hours, you will get the answer 'yes'. And instantly you will feel relieved.

You have to understand the power of this mantra and how to use it. Otherwise the question may arise that, "If it is being said to accept everything, then shouldn't we try to improve the situation? My child is not studying, my boss is not giving me a promotion, my health is not improving – so shouldn't we try to improve these circumstances?" Yes, you should definitely do so but after opening both your hands. Whenever you do not accept something, how do you work? How do you try to tackle your problems? As if you have tied one hand at the back and now you are trying to solve the problem with the other hand. This is foolishness, common sense tells us that whenever any problem arises, untie both your hands to solve the problem, it will be a lot more easier. Hence you should definitely try to improve the situation, work on the child to improve him, but first you should accept it – "Alright this is the way it is happening, I accept it. Now, what can we do?" And do that. After accepting the situation, the encounter will be more powerful and much easier for you. By doing this, you yourself will feel surprised. If you do not take the first step right, all your other steps could go wrong. That is why you have to first learn the art of acceptance and then work towards improving the situation. 'Can I accept this?' – thousands of things come into the realm of this mantra. Different incidents happen in every person's life, you have to put them in the bracket, 'Can I accept this ( )?' With acceptance, all things are absorbed easily, they do not get an enclosure to stay and so they dissolve.

How is the feeling of acceptance in children? When traveling in a train, as the train moves forward they also move forward, as it moves backwards they also move backwards. They have absolutely no resistance. But when grown-ups travel in a train, they push themselves backwards when the train moves them forward, and push themselves forward when the train moves them backwards. This way they are constantly in struggle with themselves. At the end of the journey they feel completely worn out, although they haven't done anything the whole day. Whereas when the children alight from the train, they look as fresh and happy as they were at the start of the journey. This happens due to resistance and non-acceptance in adults. They never come to terms with anything, they are constantly thinking, "I shouldn't do this…I shouldn't do that." Just look at the way they operate throughout the day! They are bound to get exhausted. From morning to night the thoughts that are crossing our minds, how do we take them? We are taking them to be hurdles thinking, "Oh! Why is this happening?…Why did this thought come to my mind?...Why did that thought come to my mind?" Or do we ever stop and put a question to ourself, "Okay, fine. Can I accept this?" The answer will come 'Yes' from within you and you will feel good. Then you will be able to handle any task at hand in an excellent manner.

Life like a river has boundaries or limitations to it, that is why a river of sorrows is created. If you remove those boundaries, the water will evaporate, the sorrows will vanish. There is so much space within us that all the miseries and sorrows can get dissolved. The misery of the whole world can dissolve and disappear, but if we put up resistance and try to stop it, then the incidents, the misery, the thoughts get an enclosure to stay inside. When you become withdrawn, you are enclosing yourself and hence the misery remains within. But with acceptance your tendency of being closed will go on diminishing and a new life will begin for you. With this new life, you will be able to take the next step. After knowing all kinds of happiness, you will find out the secret to happiness. Whenever any thought or incident troubles you when you are in a crowd or you are alone, just one question "Can I accept this?" will help you come out of that situation and you will find yourself calm and relaxed at once.

■

CHAPTER 7

SECOND STEP TO ATTAIN INSTANT HAPPINESS

'This is That what I need'

Let us understand this very important mantra for attaining instant happiness. What does it say? It says:

"Whenever and whatever thing you get in your life is **your necessity**.

What comes to you is exactly what **you need**."

On reading this mantra you would wonder as to what does it actually mean. It means that what is happening with you right now is what you need. Your mind will not agree with this. It will feel that what kind of necessity is this? This was not my need at all. But when you understand the mantra in all its aspects, then you would say that actually we are not aware as to what our needs are. What are the needs of the seekers who come here? The fact is that they themselves do not know. As soon as a seeker comes in, he asks, "Tell me what's going to happen? When will this be told and when will that be told?" Then he is told, "You will be guided in the right way. Step by step you will get whatever you need." It is crucial that certain things are not known beforehand. Yet people are caught up in the web of astrologers to know what will happen in their future. Astrologers will never prohibit them from doing that as it is their business and the only source of their livelihood. They would never want you to come out of this web.

You have come to know the truth whether your mind likes it or not. When people fill the enrollment form for Maha-Aasmani Retreat (you can read more about the retreat in the appendix), there is a question that says, "Which truth do you want – the actual truth or the one which you like?" People tick the answer that says that they want the real truth. Otherwise, the mind would like something different in the name of truth; and then will have to keep carrying it and enduring it all life long. It becomes a noose around the neck. It can neither be spit out nor swallowed. Let no one get such ignoble (*Atej*) truth. Let us get the real truth.

The events that are taking place in your life, what are they? When someone abuses you, do you say to yourself that this is exactly what I need at this moment? Do you say 'This is that what I need'?

We again will use the same symbol of a bracket ( ). Whichever context we are talking about must be written within the brackets. This symbol will also remind you of the mantra –"This is that what I need." Then whatever the matter is, whether criticism or praise, comes within the brackets. When the other person is not responding to you, there is a traffic jam, your shoes got stolen from outside the temple – are all within the brackets. This is that what I need. In short you can say – "This is That." When you wake up in the morning and there is a power cut, then you would say, "This is That," though it is not clear to you at this moment and you are doubtful whether you really need it. The mind does not agree with it. But you will say that this is the truth whether the mind agrees or not. The earlier it accepts and understands the truth, the earlier will it attain bliss. It is up to you to decide how long you want to postpone your happiness.

Don't live in the future

People are not able to live life at all. They live either in yesterday or in tomorrow. They always keep running either in the past or in the future. They are told that life is not in the past or the future, it is in the present. Many people keep postponing living their life on the pretext that they will live life some day. They spend their entire life this way. They are just unable to come to the present. The mind keeps running elsewhere – where there is no truth, where there is no present. Our attention never goes towards that. We should be careful so that, in our ignorance and unconsciousness, we don't postpone our life, we don't postpone our happiness.

Now remind yourself as to what truth you want – the one which the mind likes or the real one. Each and everyone who knew the real truth – be it the Buddha, Mahavir, Jesus, Namdeo, Eknath, Gyaneshwar, Guru Nanak, Meera, Rabia, Janabai or Dayabai – all those who attained self-realisation, have told the same truth, though the words may be different.

Those words which have become outdated today have been removed and those which are necessary today are being used. This is because the common man's language has its importance, because it is the language that people can understand and use. When one gets the knowledge and the truth in that vocabulary, they are able to relate to it in their lives. They are able to connect to it and start experimenting over it and applying it in their lives immediately. Many people are stuck in old words in religious texts, the meaning of which they don't even understand. There are quarrels and fights over those words, which have completely lost their meaning. When they will come to know the real meaning, they will be regretting over their mistake. Honest people are going to regret that they have wasted so much time over those words and that they quarrelled and fought with other people over them. Those who are able to understand the Grace and the understanding that comes with those words will be able to pay attention to that Grace and understanding. They will be able to receive the Grace and soon rise above words.

Words appear from silence, we don't get silence from words. With this conviction, silence will become most important. These words are taking us towards that realm where the prattling of the mind stops due to the inner unremitting silence (*Moun*). To prepare for that you have been told a mantra. The mantra is, "This is That what I need." On putting an incident or problem within the bracket, everything changes. As long as it was outside the bracket, it was causing trouble and distress. When we are going to accept a certain thing, if it is put within the bracket, then acceptance becomes easy. This is the miracle of the bracket; it is the miracle of that symbol shown to you. You just say 'This is That, This is that what I need," or you can just say, "This is That" since you already know the full mantra.

When someone hears this they would ask, what does it mean? (This is That?). As for you, since you know the meaning you are aware that there is an understanding associated with it, you know a secret associated with it. On the strength of this secret, you will see that these small words can yield big results. What are the words? 'This is That'. When the secret fully unfolds before you, you will say it was indeed a great truth. Let us understand this through some examples:

You are not satisfied with your present job. You are praying, "O God! Give me a bigger, better job." After some days, your boss fires you. You are shocked – you prayed for a better job and you lost even your present job. You lose faith in your prayer. At such time can you say, "This is that what I need"?

You start searching for another job and find that there is a vacancy at a good firm and they are willing to hire only those who are currently not employed anywhere else! You get the job. Now you see that being fired from your old job was your necessity, otherwise how could you have got the bigger, better job? The first scene was the preparation for the next scene.

One man was in dire need of money. He prayed for it with all his heart. Suddenly, there was an earthquake and the walls of his house started shaking. He got scared. Even his faith started to waver. He felt he is praying for money and is starting to lose even his house. He stopped praying. Had he been convinced of, 'This is that what I need," he would have realized that this was the way his prayer was being answered because his ancestors had hidden a treasure in one of the walls of the house!

A saint was going to a village with his disciples. His disciples said, "It's getting late and it will be dark by the time we reach the village. Let us stay here for the night." The saint said, "No, we will go." The disciples could not oppose him and they set off for that village. It was indeed night time when they reached there. In that village majority of the people belonged to a different sect. They were quite unwelcoming and did not provide any accommodation to them. They gave them neither food nor place to stay. All the disciples got angry as they had not wished to come there in the first place. They started complaining, "We shouldn't have come now. Where will we go at this hour?" The saint said, "Don't jump to conclusions." Whatever was happening, if only the disciples had known the mantra, they would have said, 'This is that what we need.' But they couldn't say that.

They found a ramshackle hut outside the village to spend the night. They had to sleep with all kind of hardships in that rundown place where half the roof was broken. When night set in – what a night it was!

A lovely full moon was shining in the sky with all its glory. When the saint opened his eyes after midnight, he witnessed that wonderful sight in the sky and felt so pleased that he woke up his disciples to show them too. When the disciples saw it, such feelings stirred within them, such bliss arose in them, which otherwise they would never have experienced. It was then that the disciples realised and agreed that 'This is that what we need.'

So what do we understand from this story? A few moments back it appeared that whatever was happening was wrong. They felt we certainly don't need this, we did not need to be thrown out of the village. But from the scene that came next, it was evident as to – What was the reality? What were we being prepared for? What kind of experience was to be got? What was the next scene on account of which this scene was created? The one who sees from the helicopter view (higher level of consciousness) knows this.

A little boy is going someplace. There are different paths which are winding and meandering. He is going on the wrong path, in the wrong direction in a maze from where there is no way out. He keeps getting slapped from the other side with a hand which points out – There, there. When he is being slapped, he is unable to say, 'This is That'. But when he comes out in the right direction due to that slapping, he then says, "Oh! All the slaps were for this." But while being slapped if you had asked him as to whether he felt that it was what he needed, he would have never agreed.

If you conduct a survey to check how many people on Earth had accepted when something happened to them that it was exactly what they needed, you would hardly find any. They wouldn't have accepted as an understanding is required for this. One needs courage to accept it, which comes through understanding. That courage to tread the path of Truth, as Truth is illogical. It does not seem to be correct. The mind does not accept that this would be right. What should the mind be told then? Let us assume that a situation arises where somebody steals your idea and touts it as his own. He gets full credit for it and consequent fame and success. At such time, would you be able to say, 'This is That what I need'? You would not be able to since your mind will say, "I simply cannot accept that this is what

I need." This is because you are not aware of the next scene that would happen in the future. The truth is that whatever is happening with us at this moment is for our progress and development.

We don't have to agree but just know the secret

The body in which thoughts are being produced has some quality – it has receptivity, receptivity for new ideas and thoughts, because the thoughts pass through the body. Bodies don't generate thoughts. Thoughts just pass through the body. Thoughts are coming from all sides. Thoughts see which body is transparent and deceit-free, which bodies have become eligible, which bodies have become capable – thoughts are seeing this. This is a method of explaining something which is beyond words. Actually the source of all thoughts, ideas and feelings is within us, it is within everyone of us, and it is one. It is beyond the body and the mind. It is Life, it is Consciousness, it is Self or whatever name you would like to give. Ideas arise in the body which has become eligible for them.

When there is understanding in the person whose idea got stolen, he would say "This is That" because the source of the thoughts is within me and it cannot be stolen. Hence he will have no problems with it. Mind will say, "I don't agree." Then you have to tell your mind, "Whether you agree or not, just know it." No one is asking you to agree. The mind should be told that it has never been asked to agree. It does not matter whether it agrees or not, the important thing is it should know this fact. You don't have to agree, you don't have to disagree. It has just to be known, because once you know this truth, this secret, then there is no necessity to agree. When we don't know it or understand it, then we *have* to agree because we have to begin somewhere. Therefore the mind has to be told, "Don't get stuck in this cycle of agreement and disagreement, instead just understand as this *is* the truth. Become aware at least when the next scene appears. When the event was taking place you couldn't understand; when you were stuck in the maze you couldn't understand, when you were being slapped you couldn't understand. But at least now that you are out of it, start contemplating on it. You were not aware when you were sowing the seeds of thorns, you were not ready for contemplation at that time; but now that the tree of thorns has grown out, understand and contemplate so that you won't sow the wrong seeds in the future.

Mind has to develop this habit of contemplating on the truth and on all the secrets of life before the next scene appears. Tell yourself not to get into the complication of whether to believe or not, it is vital to just know it. Understand that whenever and whatever you need, you get it. This means that whatever is happening to you now is your need and necessity. It may not be essential for someone else, but it is definitely essential for you.

Present Meditation

This book which you have got in your hand now may or may not be useful for someone else, but it is of great importance to you. People copy others' lives and actions and reject the things that come to them, in fact they throw them away. People think others are not reading this, then why am I reading; others are not doing this, why am I doing? Everybody's Gita or story is different. In accordance with your story you are building a path; and the things that you are getting now will be helpful in that path and are your necessity – the understanding, the inner experience, the bitter or sweet external experiences and the bright knowlerience (final knowledge + experience). The present is your necessity. The present is your need. What you have got in the present is your need, that is why this book has come into your hands. Otherwise people are stuck with yesterday or tomorrow and never pay any attention to the present. Hence it is important to meditate on the present, i.e. practice present meditation. Present meditation will free you from the past and future and bring you in the present.

When someone hears about such meditation, he would think that we have not heard of this before, it has not appeared in any book, it has not appeared in any Upanishad, it has not appeared in any religious book, then what is this meditation? The words chosen here are from the common man's language of today, but they will do wonders because they are new and fresh, and due to which you will not take the old meaning that usually comes with spiritual words. When you will practice with the new, bright and fresh meaning, you will see good results. When you hear such new words, you will not reject them, because you know the secret – "This is That what I need." How easily you would become flexible! When there is flexibility in your intellect, then there is receptivity for the new. Otherwise people are not ready to give up their old rituals and beliefs. And there are others who are taking advantage of this – fake saints, pundits, tricksters, magicians, wizards and the like who in order to make money and run their business keep people entangled in rituals, because they know that their brains have become numb and rigid. No one is prepared to think. People, in the guise of ancient religious practices, perform ordinary scientific marvels and cheat us saying that these are divine miracles. A sensible person will use his intellect, not get stuck with the old, get rid of outdated useless rituals, and keep his intellect flexible for receiving the Truth.

Do make use of common sense

We have to make use of our common sense when applying anything in our life. Suppose your shoes got stolen from outside a temple, and you said, "This is That what I need." Then after saying this, you have never been told not to search for your shoes. You will definitely take corrective action and put in all those efforts that are necessary on your part. You will give the appropriate response to the situation. On telling the mantra within, a feeling of acceptance has come. Now the task that will be done will be with all your intelligence, with proper and sharp intelligence. It may then click you that someone has worn your shoes by mistake. Otherwise, the brain loaded with stress cannot even think. Therefore you have to understand the meaning of what is being told and also how to apply it using common sense.

It definitely does not mean that you have to accept the situation as your need and then sit with folded hands. This has been happening in spirituality. When people are told one thing, they hold on to something different. Those who don't want to study, those who don't want to work will find some excuse. Those who want to run away from responsibilities also use the truth as an excuse. Thinking themselves to be wise, they use words of wisdom to support their tendency of laziness. They will use opium and other drugs and try to justify it by saying that such-and-such a saint also used to consume them. If that saint had known earlier, he would have told them the reason in advance or would have quit consuming it. If he had known that people would be using his name later for doing such things, he would definitely have quit himself. These individuals never tried to understand why that saint used to smoke; they have just found an excuse to smoke in the name of spirituality. Now they will continue to live with that deception.

Ask yourself honestly whether you want to walk the path of truth or use the truth as an excuse. Those who have used the truth as an excuse for their bad habits are the ones who have corrupted the truth. The Buddha preached some things, but people in accordance to their whims have corrupted it. That which was never told by the Buddha, Mahavir or other great saints was practised by some people because these people had nothing to do with the truth. They needed the words of truth for conveniently and safely perpetuating their tendencies and their ego. When you are walking the path of truth, when you are using the mantra of truth, always ask yourself honestly whether you are doing it because you really want to walk the path of truth or do you just want to cover up your laziness or other vices?

Definitely make use of common sense. You will become aware and alert.

Understand the secret of prayer

You are waiting for the lift and the lift is not coming down, you would say, "This is That what I need." Until the lift comes, what will you do? As soon as you have said the mantra, you can practice the present meditation and come in the present. You look around to see what is there that is awe-inspiring and instantly come in the present. Otherwise the mind will keep running between the past and the future. Man prays, "O God! Give me patience" and the lift does not come. He does not realize that this is the fruit of his prayer. Whenever you are waiting in a queue, be it for rations, for tickets, for payment of bills, just ask yourself as to what you had prayed for. This is the arrangement in answer to your prayer. In what a beautiful way your prayers are being fulfilled. But if someone doesn't know the secret of prayer, and straightaway you tell him that whatever is happening is the answer to his own prayers, he will get very upset with you.

If you want to develop patience, certain events will occur for making you patient. Otherwise what do you expect to happen when you pray for patience? Will flowers be showered on you from the heavens? Such things are told in stories to make children understand as to what will happen. The prayer you are doing is, "O God! I want courage." Then what will happen in your life? Someone will come and frighten you. You will say 'Yes' i.e. this was what you needed, because this occurrence was necessary for you to develop courage. You will then take it as a challenge and will soon see that you have got the courage which you wanted. But if at that time you have forgotten the secret, then you will become very miserable. Waves of fear agitate you so much, your blood pressure is affected, everything gets messed up; you become sick. You totally forget that due to which prayer this has happened. Just visualize as to how a person's life would be if he knows all the secrets of life. For the one who knows all the secrets and is fully convinced about them, how would he be living his life? It would be a life full of happiness.

Strong faith should to be copied

How easily Jesus went on the cross! What was the understanding he had? That is the understanding that we have to receive. We should copy the strong faith that he had. People copy external things. They copy the external attributes of a movie star, but do they copy the confidence and the conviction that is present within them? We should get that confidence and conviction. In whichever field you want to progress, you should copy the conviction of the successful people in that field. People copy external styles such as the manner of smoking, the cell phones, clothes, accessories and the like. But they don't develop self-confidence from all these things, though they may get the illusion of confidence for some time. What level of self-confidence is present in the ones who have attained final wisdom (Tejgyan)! What conviction is there in devotees! What conviction of devotion is present in devotees! What kind of conviction of love was present inside Meera! Let that percolate within us.

This mantra, this secret, this understanding is to open you up, to remove the constriction and closedness in you and to make you look at each incident in a proper perspective. With what eyes would you see? See with the fourth eye. Till now how have we been seeing? Now when an incident will take place – you are waiting for something – but that waiting also will give you happiness. If waiting is not giving you happiness, then you have forgotten something. You have to remind yourself as to what is it that you have forgotten – the mantra, the understanding – and then you know this incident is appearing to be troublesome because you forgot such and such things. As soon as you remember it, you will feel happy; the lift will also come.

What response needs to be given for that which is in the present

You are going someplace and there is a traffic jam or the road is blocked. How irritated you get! And when someone overtakes you from the side, how you curse him! But now that you know the mantra, you would say, 'This is That what I need.' If you happen to meet that person later on the road ahead, you would thank him because he gave you an opportunity to apply your understanding and develop patience in you. (It is not necessary that he understands why you have thanked him). In this way, several different incidents are taking place in your life and you can apply the wisdom you have attained and be happy.

If someone breaks some article of yours, you will instantly feel anger arising within you, but when you remember the mantra, then what would you say? And also see if it is possible to repair the broken article. Certainly think as to what is the appropriate response to the situation. You will definitely think as to what can be done for making amends, but first say, 'This is That' and after remembering the mantra you will go ahead with an open mind. How many people have come to this Earth and died having collected thousands of antique pieces, so what is the point in that? They get distressed if even a small object gets broken, and also become emotional – my greeting card, my gift which my late friend had given me, my antique piece… and keep fighting over it with others – others who are living conscious people. They keep weeping over those who lived yesterday and quarreling with those who are living today. If they have understanding, they will say 'This is That' mantra is there to teach a lesson. What is important is to learn as to what response is to be given to those who are there with us at present. In this way, you will progress ahead.

You saw an acquaintance on the way, but he went away without even giving you a smile. You will say, "This is That what I need.

I don't know what he needs, but this is what I needed." Someone does not even greet you with a hello, does not ask you about your welfare, having gone to a party no one asks whether you ate or not, there is no food left and you have nothing to eat. Then you say, 'This is That what I need.' If fasting was what was needed for you, then you will go on a fast for the night. Otherwise you will be tossing in bed all night long and thinking – no food was left for me, while others had delicious food for themselves, family members had gone to the hotel and had yummy food, and what did they bring for me? They said, "Oh! We thought you must have eaten at the party and so we did not get you anything." Now you are so upset that you can't stop tossing in the bed thinking, 'No one pays any attention to me, no one loves me…' But now if you know the mantra, you will say, 'This is That', today fasting is essential for me and hence this has happened. You can then go to sleep without having to bear all those torturing thoughts.

Small things can do big miracles for you. As said earlier, do make use of common sense, if some eatable can be bought or prepared or if milk is available, then drink it. Don't say that 'I am fasting, so I won't even drink milk.' Don't torment your body unnecessarily. In the name of spirituality people sleep even on nails and do all kinds of incredible but useless things. Hence it is said that if you apply this secret in your life with understanding, then you will enjoy it.

Somebody else is having the remote control to your TV and is changing the channels, and you are just watching. Not knowing which channel he would like that you will have to watch, you just sit and say, 'This is That.' In this way in each situation, be it a cricket or football match where your country wins or loses, you say, 'This is That what I need' and hence not break the TV. Look at the condition of people after defeat, how miserable and upset they are! People keep discussing about this in the newspapers, in the neighbourhood and in the office. How much of time is being wasted! You never ever thought about how you could have hit a boundary or scored a goal. You would get a jolt if you think how you can make a goal. If you have never thought about your goal, then the time has come to make a goal, the time has come to know the secret, the time has come to take a challenge, and the time has come to show your courage.

■

CHAPTER 8

THIRD STEP TO ATTAIN INSTANT HAPPINESS

'Can I convert it into a ladder'

Here is the next step to attain happiness. Ask yourself, "Can I convert it into a ladder?" This means that whatever is the situation, can I convert it into a ladder? Can I use it for my development, can I use it for my total self development? In the classical board game of snakes and ladders, you go up the ladder and come down a snake. Self transformation and attaining happiness becomes easy if you have learnt to convert every snake into a ladder. You may encounter obstacles on the path. Let the obstacles not become excuses. Transform every obstacle into an instrument for growth and every snake into a ladder. In every adverse situation ask yourself, "Can I turn the snakes into ladders?" You will be astonished to learn that actually every snake can be converted into a ladder.

Spiritualism teaches you that the world is a game of snakes and ladders and spiritualism is the knowledge to convert snakes into ladders. To convert snakes into ladders implies how to make use of even a negative thought that arises in the mind or a negative incident that has occured. You have accepted it and also said 'This is That', that is fine, but these are just the first steps. There is one more step – to learn something from that incident. This is what will help you attain your goal of self development, success and happiness. Self development signifies the knowledge of converting the snakes into ladders. The snakes in our life are depression, stress, worry and anger that prevent us from getting true happiness. These can be converted into ladders to attain happiness.

Some people are depressed in life and on top of that they feel unhappy about that depression as well. They are always thinking, "Why am I so depressed?" But they are told "Congratulations." Why the congratulations? Because this is important, those who get depressed are the ones who become seekers. You will come to know that depression makes you move forward in life. You try to find out : What is the ultimate truth? Why do we become miserable? What is the reason? Can we change our thoughts? Is there something permanent and steady within us? Where should we search for it? With what perspective should we look at life? Questions like these can start your quest for the truth.

So don't get scared when depression sets in. You are stressed out and you worry about it as to why you are stressed, i.e. stress upon stress. This is wrong. Some people when they feel angry get more furious thinking as to why they became angry – 'Why did I get angry? I shouldn't have got angry…' It is okay to be angry, it is alright, but anger upon your anger is harmful. If you just understand that we don't have to get angry over our anger or depressed upon our depression, it will be great. If depression has set in, let us see what will it do, where will it take us. It has definitely come to make us do something which is essential for our growth. Later in life you will say, "It's good that I got depressed. It is due to that depression that I have progressed and attained the truth and happiness." Those who never get distressed, never achieve anything great in life. They always remain mediocre.

■

CHAPTER 9

LEARNING MORE ABOUT ACCEPTING

- Can I accept this?
- Isn't this that what I exactly need now?
- How can I covert this into a ladder?

These three questions shall result in "accepting" the problem or situation. They are three powerful strategies of "accepting". You should give yourself an opportunity to experience every one of them and thus explore the power and wisdom they contain. Each strategy then becomes a handy tool that will help you face any situation, shape any event, avoid misery and derive happiness out of it, which is our ultimate aim. Since accepting is such an important topic, let us understand it in further detail.

Why Accepting works

Acceptance works because it changes your mindset instantly. When we face a problem, it immediately generates negative feelings. We attempt to somehow get out of it as quickly as possible. But whatever we do, standing on the platform of negative feelings shall not work. Actions based on negative feelings only make the situation worse.

When things don't work, we think that taking more actions shall solve it now. Or maybe blaming someone else will. This simply results in further complications. What could have been done easily and effortlessly becomes a huge tidal wave of effort that does not yield any result. What is just an 'ant' now becomes a 'tyrant'.

There are many who go for a job interview, though they have a job in hand. They do it just to find their market value. The same people report that if for some reason they lose their job and then go for an interview, then they usually make a mess out of the interview. They stutter or stammer their way through. Why? This is because the second interview is given standing on the platform of negative feelings of fear, worry or insecurity. It only generates negative energy all the more.

When we accept the situation using any of the above three questions, this negative platform is demolished. The vortex of negative energy does not arise. In addition, we experience mental clarity. New avenues that were not visible earlier now become visible. Learners of a new language usually go though an important step before they become fluent in what they are attempting. They tell themselves it is alright to make mistakes. The moment they do this, they become bolder and better in the new language. If they haven't undergone this step, then they just focus on mistakes. The more they focus on mistakes, the more mistakes they make. Accepting stops this over-pushing and focusing on the negative.

The moment you accept the situation, it helps you in the following ways:

a. Built in negative energy dissipates.

b. Your focus changes from "what is wrong" to "what could be improved now."

c. The mind becomes clearer and calmer.

d. You become more single minded and focused. Other distractions diminish.
e. You see new avenues not visible earlier. The fog on the overall picture dissipates.
f. Your decision making ability is enhanced.
g. You feel more balanced emotionally.
h. Your irritation fades away or you get relief from a disturbed state of mind.
i. You unconsciously begin to reframe the words. What was irritating is now just a small botheration. Thus your experience of life changes.
j. You feel freer to handle the situation at hand without the extra emotional and mental baggage.
k. The energy which was being consumed by your feelings of fear, worry or anger is saved. Thus you have this extra energy at your disposal, which you can use for solving the given situation with renewed vigour as well as for other constructive purposes.

Acceptance does not mean running away from the situation

Many people misunderstand acceptance as running away from a situation. Acceptance is not about fleeing. It is about flying. It is about taking flight because you are no longer chained by negative energy. Acceptance does not mean you stop desiring or aiming for more or for something else. An aim provides direction. Accepting that we may not reach some milestones helps us to decide newer avenues to reach the aim. It does not make us quit the road altogether. Not accepting the situation can mean that we choose the wrong road or maybe even retard our journey.

The Bhagwad Gita tells us about dispassionate action. Most people question how to be dispassionate. Acceptance does precisely that. What it does is that it stops you from being too emotionally attached to your aim. Acceptance moves you from yearning for your aim to focusing on your aim. It moves you from forcing yourself to freeing yourself to act the way a situation demands. You want to go to sleep at night. It is alright to have such an aim. But if you force yourself to sleep, you shall never get sleep. Instead you tell yourself it is alright if I don't sleep. Can I accept that I am not able to sleep? The moment you stop resisting it, you shall fall asleep.

An important law of life is that whatever you resist shall persist. If you are resisting your not being able to achieve your aim or resisting your not getting promoted – it shall persist. Why? Because the law that what you resist shall persist is a corollary to the law that what you focus on multiplies in your life. When you resist the negative outcome, you actually focus on the negative and attract the negative. When you accept the negative, you no longer resist it and are free from it. Thus accepting is not about running away from the outcome but it is about choosing a new outcome or a new avenue for an outcome because you are no longer constrained by negative energy caused by resisting, forcing, yearning or the like.

Acceptance causes giant shifts in your consciousness

Another law of life is that what is true at one level is true at all levels. As in small, so in big. As in the microcosm, so in the macrocosm. When you answer "Yes" to the "Can I accept this?" question, then you have let go of negative feelings associated with it. You may think that this is just a small step. But when you do so, it causes a giant shift in your consciousness. At that very moment, lot of other unrelated things open up for you and you begin to attract more positive things. The moment you let go of a negative feeling through acceptance, you are telling your subconscious mind that I am open to the abundance of the universe. I am not going to cringe like a miser. Then the law, 'What you focus on multiplies in your life' takes over. The smallest letting go action helps us in every facet of our life. Not only do you become mentally free, but it affects you at the physical, emotional, social and financial level too. It sets off a chain reaction that reverberates through our entire being and leaves us in quite a different place than we were before the acceptance.

How do you use this knowledge that even a small act of acceptance causes a giant shift in consciousness? Simple. Whenever you find yourself troubled by a huge problem, accept something small related either to the problem or anything else. This small shift will help you tackle the bigger one easily too.

How do you know you have accepted?

In chemistry, a litmus test is used to decide whether a solution is acidic or not. A litmus is a special type of filter paper that turns red under acidic conditions. It is a test to see if the chemical reaction intended was successful or not and whether acid was produced or not. Similarly, is there any such test that tells you whether your acceptance was successful or not? There is. When you have accepted something, the problem or situation seems different. So, how do you apply the litmus test? Simple. After having accepted, review the situation in your mind. See the problem again. If your acceptance has worked, it usually does, then the problem or situation seems lighter and clearer. If there is still some negative emotion left over, again accept by asking, "Can I accept this?" Again see the situation in your mind. Has it lightened? Keep doing so till you are fully clear.

Instead of using, "Can I accept this?", you could use the other two questions too. In fact "Isn't this that what I need" is an even more powerful question that you could replace in the litmus test above. How can I convert it into a ladder, also immediately results in releasing negative blockages. You shall gain something from the problem, instead of losing something due to it. In this way you begin to look at a problem from a positive point of view. If you are looking at a problem positively, then how is it a "problem"? This understanding will shift your view permanently about "problems" of life and their "purpose". This shifting shall give you instant happiness whenever you have to face any problem henceforth in you life. Because now you know what to do and what to feel.

■

CHAPTER 10

PRACTICAL STEPS FOR ACCEPTING

Let us now apply "accepting" to various situations in life and practically understand it.

Accepting the past

"If only" are two words that make many miserable. "If only I hadn't failed." "If only I hadn't married." "If only I were more careful." An action or inaction in the past causes strong negative emotions. Many are not even aware that most of their present actions are just an attempt to change the past. You can't change the past. You can accept the past and alter your present instead. The best way to let go of your past is through accepting. Another negative oft repeated question is "why". "Why didn't I do this?" "Why didn't I do that?" A better idea is to change the "why" to "how". "How can I convert it into a ladder?" is a super question that helps you convert your follies into stepping stones.

Whenever you find yourself lamenting about the past or repenting about something in the past, apply either of the following strategies:

a. Ask yourself, "Can I accept my past?" This question alone may be enough.

b. Yet, if you find yourself brooding again and again over the past, then analyse how what happened in the past was something you actually "required" for today or for the future.

c. Ask yourself, "Is there something from the incident of the past that I could use as a ladder for the future?"

You shall get an answer. Getting an answer to any or all of these questions usually helps in unburdening the past.

Accepting an uncertain future

Many of us harbour "fear" about our future instead of planning our future. Aspiring for something is different from being anxious about something. If you are anxious, nervous or fearful of some incident about the future, then you are unconsciously attracting a negative future. Remember the law of life: "Whatever you focus on multiplies in your life." To get rid of focusing on the negative in the future, accept the future. See the event happening in the future in your mind. Usually you fear a negative consequence of the event. Ask yourself the question, "Can I accept this event or situation, as it is, without wanting to change or control the event?" Notice that the question has changed. You are not asked to see the negative consequence and then accept it. You are asked here to let go of over-wanting to control your future. You can desire to control or change your future. But don't over-push or over-want.

Let us say you are awaiting the results of an examination. You are uncertain about what shall happen and are very anxious. See the day of the results in your mind. Ask yourself, "Can I accept whatever that is going to happen that day without wanting to change it?" This shall usually provide you with a huge relief.

Accepting negative feelings

Feelings are useful tools. Even negative ones. Don't suppress negative feelings. Don't explode either. There is a middle path. Express your negative feelings. There are times you cannot or may not want to express. Then accept them. You shall also notice that once you accept your negative feelings, you feel free to talk about it, to express it. If you suppress it, it usually comes back later. If you explode, then you feel further negative feelings of guilt. Expression is the best way. Acceptance is the spring board on which you can express. If required, you can take action based on your negative feeling. But only after you accept it and neutralize your feeling. Any action taken standing on the platform of a negative feeling is usually counter-productive and backfires. What works is to be complete with the event that caused the negative feeling, neutralize the feeling through accepting it and then express or take action if required.

The first step is to identify the feeling by giving it a name. All negative feelings are usually based on three basic feelings: unhappiness (being sad), anger (being mad) or fear (being scared). A sample list including such feelings that can be categorised under these three basic feelings as well as those that cannot be categorised under any of the three is given below:

Unhappiness (Being Sad)	Anger (Being Mad)	Fear (Being Scared)	Others (Mixed Feelings)
Dejected	Annoyed	Afraid	Ashamed
Depressed	Disgusted	Anxious	Bored
Disappointed	Frustrated	Apprehensive	Confused
Discouraged	Furious	Frightened	Defeated
Helpless	Hateful	Insecure	Doubtful
Hopeless	Hostile	Intimidated	Guilty
Hurt	Irritated	Nervous	Overwhelmed
Unloved	Used	Terrified	Torn
Worthless	Vengeance	Vulnerable	Unsure

Once you identify the feeling, ask yourself the question, "Can I accept the feeling as it is without wanting to change it?" Accept that feeling and just be with it. As it is. Be with it how much ever you can. Then it shall vanish. Maybe another feeling will surface. Accept it and be with it too. Till you reach a peaceful state. What happens is that the feeling gets released and you are left in a relaxed, no-mind, peaceful state. That is because feelings are closest to the source, the Self, where the feeling of peace and state of no-mind exists. When you truly dive deep into your feeling by accepting it, you reach the Self – you reach consciousness, emptiness, sheer happiness.

When you do this, the feeling is released from you without you having to suppress it. Don't fight the feelings. Many become angry and then become angry on being angry. This is called as double anger. Many become depressed that they are depressed. This is double depression. All you have to do is to accept the anger or depression or any other feeling, as it is. Don't resist it. What you resist, shall persist. Accept it and be with it till it vanishes.

Accepting pain or illness

Accepting is very useful during times of pain or illness. Whenever there is pain, there is the real physical pain and the associated mental pain. When you ask yourself the question, "Can I accept the pain?", what you do is that you let go of the mental pain. This means 50% or more of the pain is gone. The body can handle the physical pain. Accepting can help in small pains fading off completely too. (Of course, any major pain or any illness needs medical intervention). Remember, you are not avoiding the pain. You are only telling the truth about the pain and hence the psychosomatic component of it disappears.

Accepting in relationships

Accepting is most useful in relationships, be it between a husband and wife or parent and child. When you accept a person as he/

she is, the relationship improves significantly. The trick is to accept the qualities you are most irritated about. Instead of asking the question, "Can I accept the person?", it is better to ask the question, "Can I accept his/her chewing nails?" Thus accept bit by bit till you accept completely. Remember when you accept someone's negative behaviour, you are not condoning it. You still can and should communicate about it. But your communication after acceptance shall be devoid of any negative emotion and hence shall cause better impact.

What to do if it is difficult to accept

1. Try to 'accept' again and again. Ask the question repeatedly.

2. Try other accepting questions other than "Can I accept this?"

3. Accept not being able to accept it. This is a very critical step. Ask yourself, "Can I accept that I cannot accept it?"

4. Accept only the negative feeling that the situation is causing by identifying the feeling.

5. Accept only some part of the situation. Accept bit by bit. This will help in complete acceptance.

All the practical hints of acceptance described above will help you get rid of any negative feelings associated with any situation or person and guide you towards the path of joy and happiness.

∎

CHAPTER 11

SUMMARY

The objective of this book was to take some steps towards attaining instant happiness, to work on the three mantras, particularly the first and the second. Some people are absolutely closed due to fears. They feel that if they go in the dark, someone might catch them, or they fear going to any new place. For such people a mantra is given : "I am God's property, no evil can touch me." (You can repeat this mantra in any language of your preference). This mantra or maxim is for those people who have fear instilled in their hearts, and because of their fears they are not able to open up. They have to repeat this mantra constantly. Words, mantras, have power in them. In the ancient times, when blessings or curses were uttered, they used to actualize. Hence when you repeat the mantra, 'I am God's property, no evil can touch me, no unfavorable occurrence can affect me,' you will find that your tendency of being withdrawn and closed due to fear will stop altogether.

The main purpose of this book should be clear to you. You were told about seven different kinds of happiness. The main purpose is that after attaining the fifth and the sixth kind, we should attain the seventh kind of happiness. It is then that we come to know our real self and experience our sense of being which has been described as self-realization in words (actually words cannot describe that state). The happiness that we attain after realizing our true Self is the seventh kind of happiness.

To attain real happiness, you will have to come out of your shell, your tendency of being closed. And you will have to go to the place of your origin, your source (Tejasthan) [2]. The pathway to Tejasthan is the mantra of acceptance – 'Can I accept this? Whatever is happening, can I accept it?' With this many doors will open to you and your tendency of being closed will cease. You were made to perform the exercise of spreading out your arms with the help of which you will open up and get the taste of happiness. Do this exercise regularly when you are alone at home or in your bathroom, wherever you find it possible – just let go of your inhibitions and open up. After that the joy that emanates from opening up will be there for you to feel.

The mantra of 'This is That' revealed a very important secret of life. It will totally change your perspective of looking at the incidents and problems that take place in your life. It will abolish your unhappiness over unwanted situations and take you towards a higher level of happiness. The third mantra 'Can I convert it into a ladder?' will help you convert even negative occurrences into positive ones.

Till date, many things, situations and opportunities have come your way. Do not get confused or entangled in the outward appearance of the opportunity; recognize the opportunity. If this wisdom, this knowledge has reached you, then you should be concerned only about how you can take maximum advantage of it and how you can receive the great mantra of truth that will change your life forever

---

[2] *Tejasthan signifies the place within us where the Universal Self connects with the human body, which is taken to be roughly in the area of the heart.*

by attending the Maha Aasmani Retreat. After the Maha Aasmani Retreat, you will find yourself waking up to a new kind of morning every day. Each day, you will wake up twice in the mornings. Until now you have been waking up only once, but during the Maha Aasmani Retreat you will learn the art of waking up twice. You will acquire the knack of awakening in the Truth, of awakening in bliss.

♦ ♦ ♦

You can mail your opinion or feedback on this book to:
books.feedback@tejgyan.org

APPENDICES

About Sirshree

Sirshree's spiritual quest, which began during his childhood, led him on a journey through various schools of philosophy and meditation practices. He studied a wide range of literature on mind science and spirituality. After a long period of deep contemplation on the truth of life, his quest culminated in attaining the ultimate truth.

Sirshree espouses, "All spiritual paths that lead to the truth begin differently but culminate at the same point – Understanding. This understanding is complete in itself. Listening to this understanding is enough to attain the Truth." Over the last two decades, he has dedicated his life to raising mass consciousness.

Sirshree has delivered more than 4000 discourses that throw light on this understanding. He has designed a system for wisdom, which makes it accessible to all. This system has inspired people from all walks of life to progress on their journey of the Truth. Thousands of seekers join in a virtual prayer for World Peace and Global Healing daily at 9:09 am and 9:09 pm.

About Tej Gyan Foundation

Tej Gyan Foundation is a non-profit organization founded on the teachings of Sirshree. The Foundation disseminates Tejgyan – the wisdom that guides one from self-development to Self-realization, leading towards Self-stabilization.

The Foundation's system for imparting wisdom has been assessed by international quality auditors and accredited with the ISO 9001:2015 certification. This wisdom has been presented in a simple, systematic, and practically applicable form that makes it accessible to people from all walks of life, regardless of religion, caste, social strata, country, or belief system.

The Foundation has centers in more than 400 cities and towns across India and other countries. The mission of Tej Gyan Foundation is to create a highly evolved society by leading seekers from negative to positive thoughts and further, from positive thoughts to Happy thoughts. A 'Happy thought' is the auspicious thought of being free from all thoughts, leading to the state of supreme bliss beyond thoughts.

If you seek such wisdom that leads you beyond mere knowledge, dissolves all problems, frees you from all limiting beliefs, reveals the true nature of divinity, and establishes you in the ultimate truth, then it is time to discover Tejgyan; it is time to rise above the mundane knowledge of words and experience Tejgyan!

The MahaAasmani Magic of Awakening Retreat

Self-development to Self-realization towards Self-stabilization

Do you wish to experience unconditional happiness that is not dependent on any reason? Happiness that is permanent and only increases with time? Do you wish to experience love, peace, self-belief, harmony in relationships, prosperity, and true contentment? Do you wish to progress in all facets of your life, viz. physical, mental, social, financial, and spiritual?

If you seek answers to these questions and are thirsty for the ultimate truth, then you are welcome to participate in the MahaAasmani Magic of Awakening retreat organized by Tej Gyan Foundation. This is the Foundation's flagship retreat based on the teachings of Sirshree.

The Purpose of this Retreat

The purpose of this retreat is that every human being should:

- Discover the answer to "Who am I" and "Why am I?" through direct experience and be established in ultimate bliss.

- Learn the art of living in the present, free from the burden of the past and the anxiety of the future.

- Acquire practical tools to help quieten the chattering mind and dissolve problems.

- Discover missing links in the practices of Meditation (*Dhyana*), Action (*Karma*), Wisdom (*Gyana*), and Devotion (*Bhakti*).

About Books by Sirshree

Sirshree's published work includes more than 150 book titles, some of which have been translated into more than 10 languages. His literature provides a profound reading on various topics of practical living and unravels the missing links in karma, wisdom, devotion, meditation, and consciousness.

His books have been published by leading publishing houses like Penguin, Hay House, Bloomsbury, Wisdom Tree, Jaico, etc. "The Source" book series, authored by Sirshree, has sold over 10 million copies. Various luminaries and celebrities like His Holiness the Dalai Lama, publishers Mr. Reid Tracy, Ms. Tami Simon and Yoga Master Dr. B. K. S. Iyengar have released Sirshree's books and lauded his work.

The Source
Attain Both, Inner Peace
and Worldly success

Awaken the Power of Faith
Discover the 7 Principles of the
Highest Power of the Universe

To order books authored by Sirshree, login to:
www.gethappythoughts.org
For further details, call: +91 9011013210

Tej Gyan Foundation – Contact details

Registered Office:
Happy Thoughts Building, Vikrant Complex, Near Tapovan Mandir, Pimpri, Pune 411017, INDIA. Contact: +91 20-27411240, +91 20-27412576

MaNaN Ashram:
Survey No. 43, Sanas Nagar, Nandoshi Gaon, Kirkatwadi Phata, Off Sinhagad Road, Taluka Haveli, Pune district - 411024, INDIA. Contact: +91 992100 8060.

WORLD PEACE PRAYER

Divine Light of Love, Bliss, and Peace is Showering;
The Golden Light of Higher Consciousness is Rising;
All negativity on Earth is Dissolving;
Everyone is in Peace and Blissfully Shining;
O God, Gratitude for Everything!

Members of Tej Gyan Foundation have been offering this impersonal mass prayer for many years. Those who are happy can offer this prayer. Those feeling low or suffering from illness can receive healing with this prayer.

If you are feeling troubled or sick, please sit to receive the healing effect of this prayer. Visualize that the divine white healing light is being showered on earth through the prayers of thousands and is also reaching you, bringing you peace and good health. You can dwell in this feeling for some time and then offer your gratitude to those offering the prayer.

A Humble Appeal

More than a million peace lovers are praying for World Peace and Global Healing every morning and evening at 9:09. This prayer is also webcast on YouTube at 9:00 pm. Please participate in this noble endeavor.

www.ingramcontent.com/pod-product-compliance
Lightning Source LLC
LaVergne TN
LVHW041542070526
838199LV00046B/1796